THESE FOOLISH THINGS REMIND ME OF YOU

Niina Lehtonen Braun

KERBER ART

THESE FOOLISH THINGS
REMOIND ME
OF YOU:

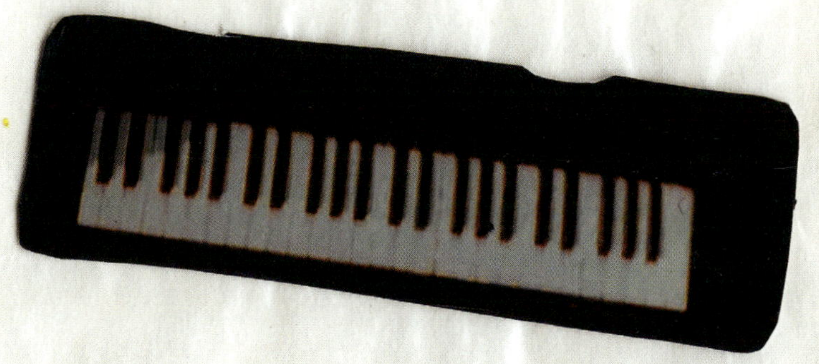

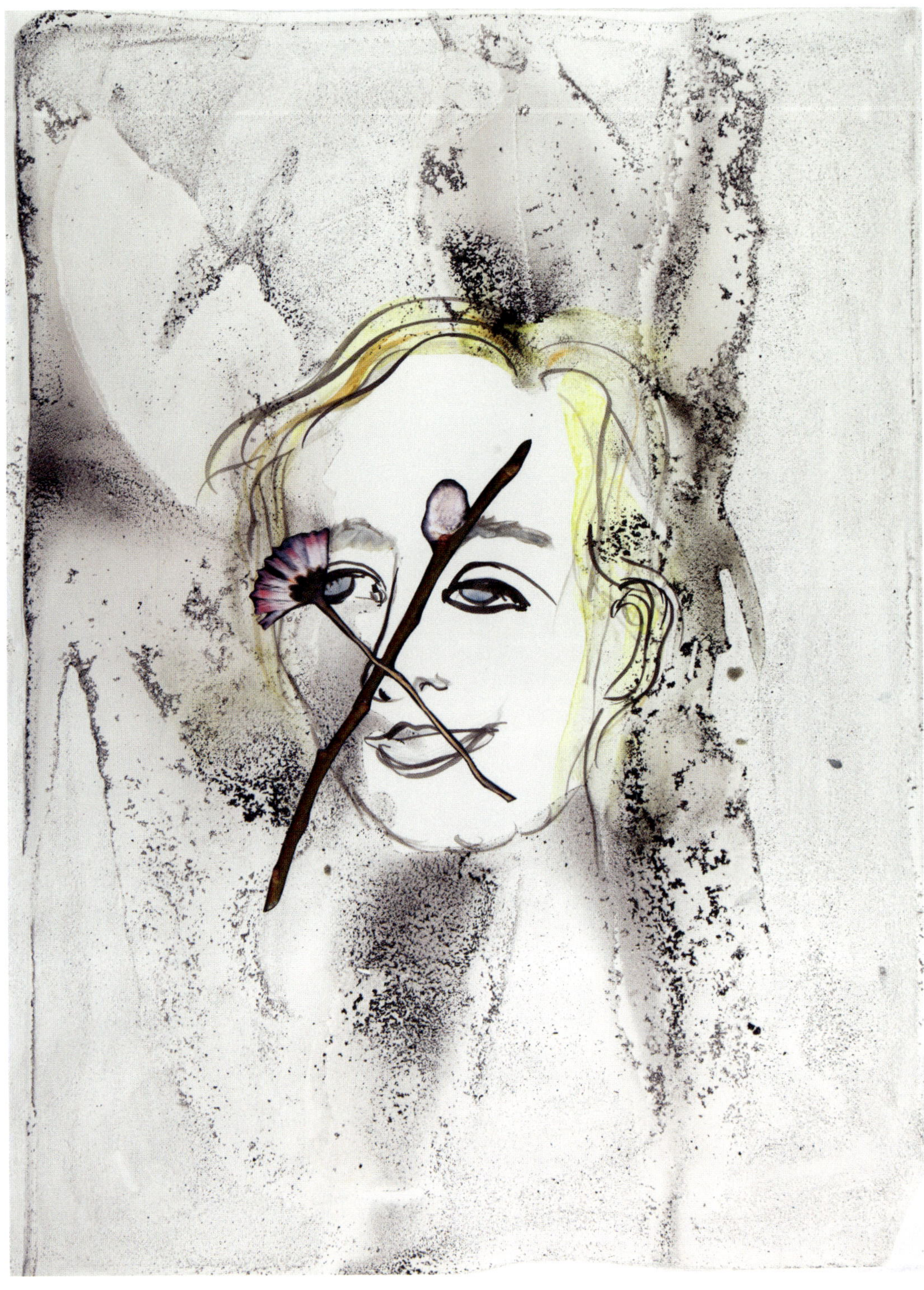

DRIED BANANAS
REMIND ME OF
MY GRANDAD. I SAT
ON HIS KNEES AND
PRETENDED TO SMOKE
CIGARS WITH HIM.
I LOVED HIM DEARLY
UNTIL I FOUND OUT
HE WAS A TERRIBLE
RIGHTWING NATIONALIST
IF NOT FASCIST.

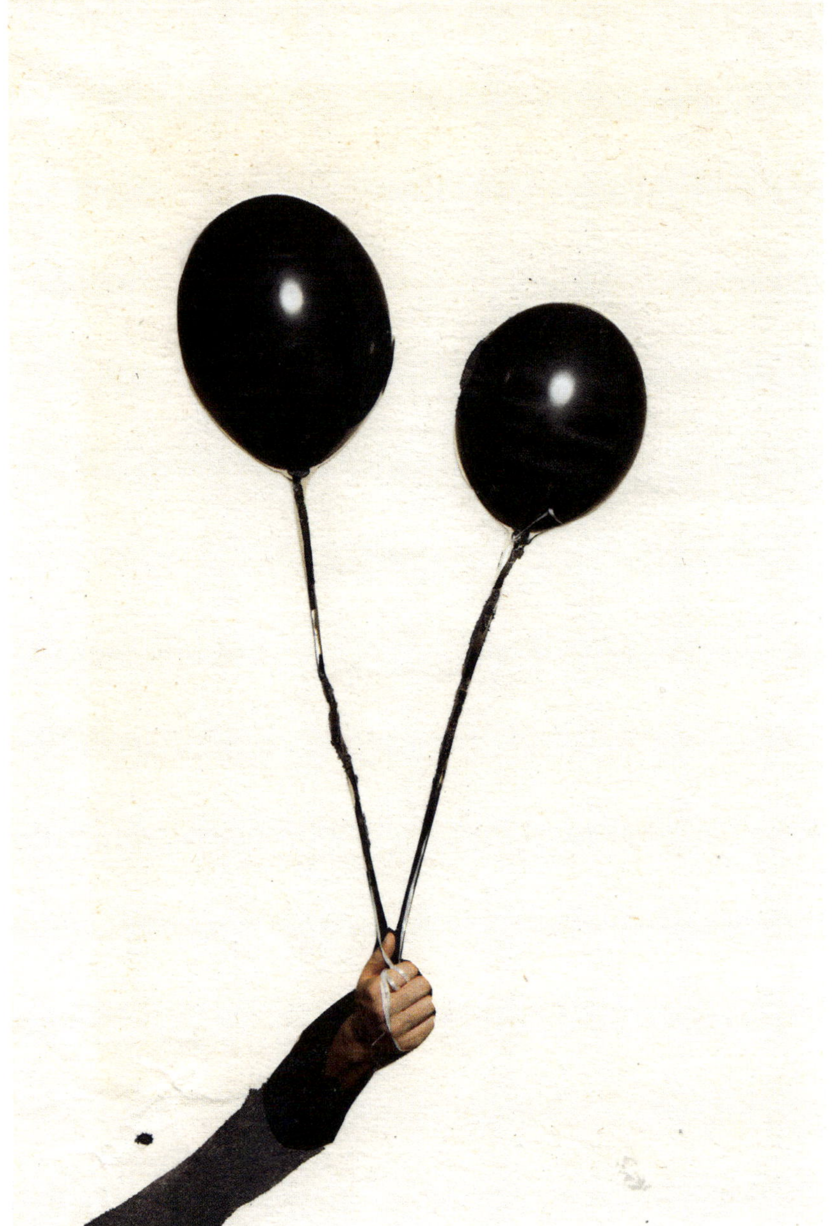

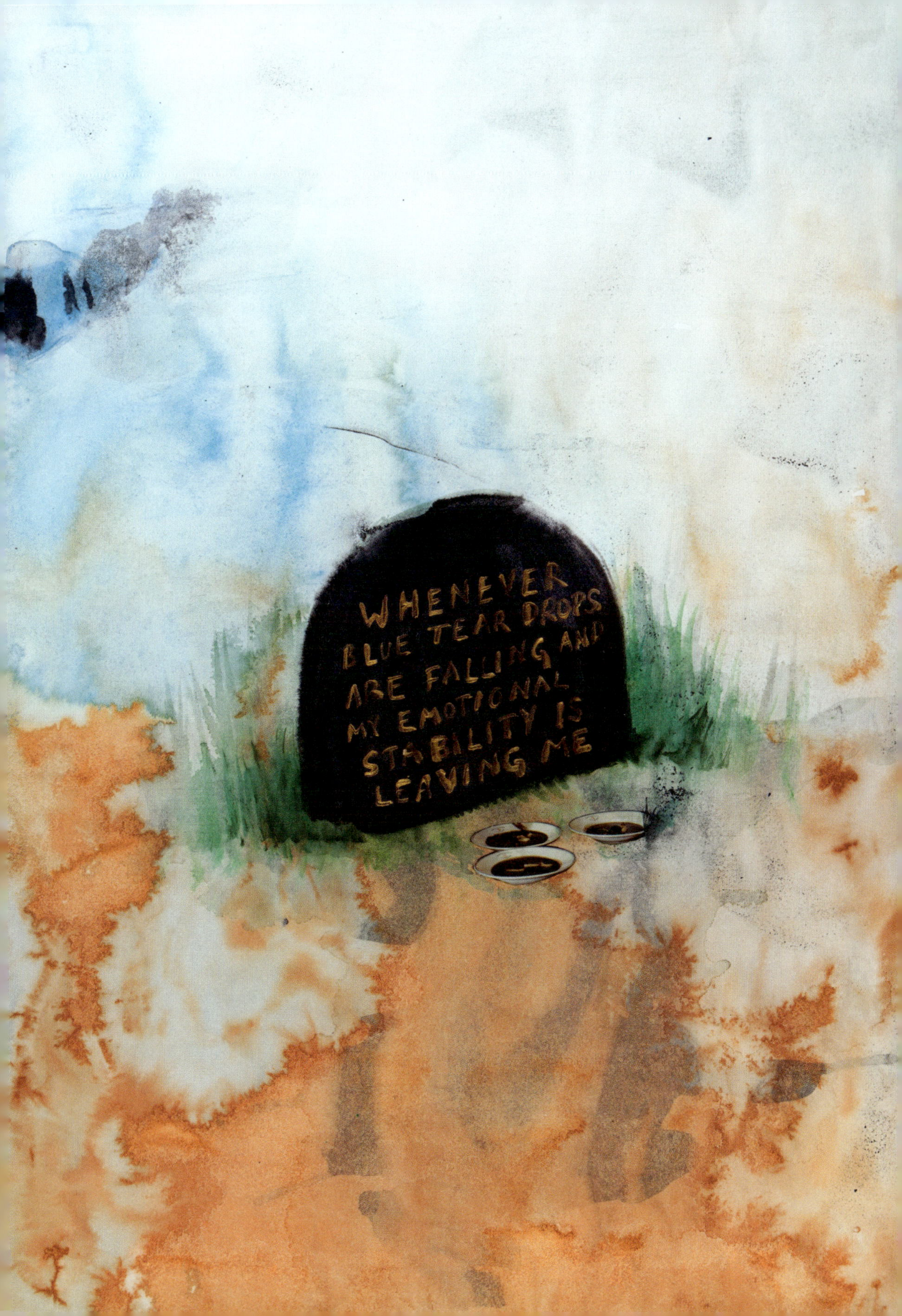

WHENEVER
BLUE TEAR DROPS
ARE FALLING AND
MY EMOTIONAL
STABILITY IS
LEAVING ME

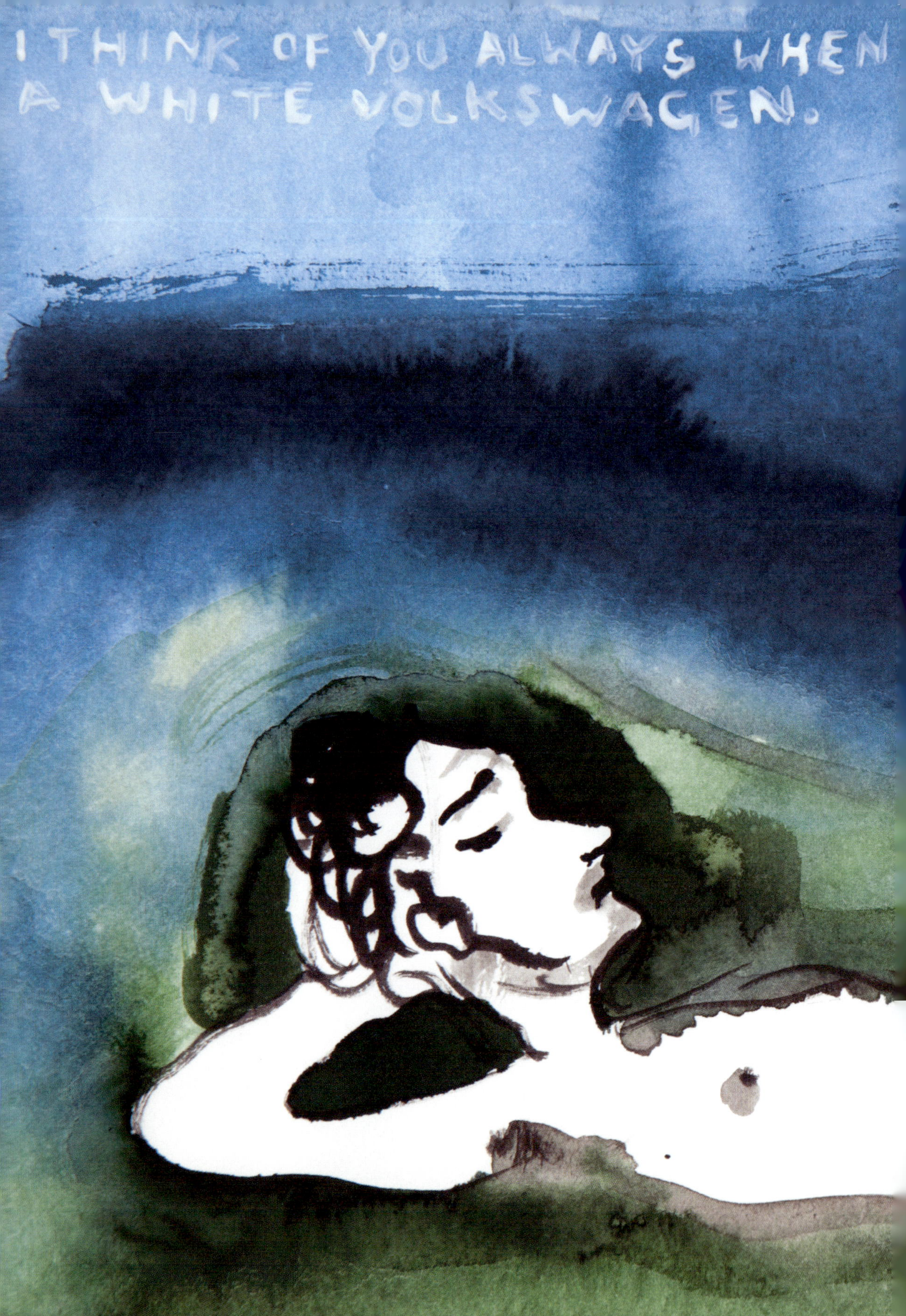
I THINK OF YOU ALWAYS WHEN
A WHITE VOLKSWAGEN.

SEE A CONSTRUCTION SITE OR

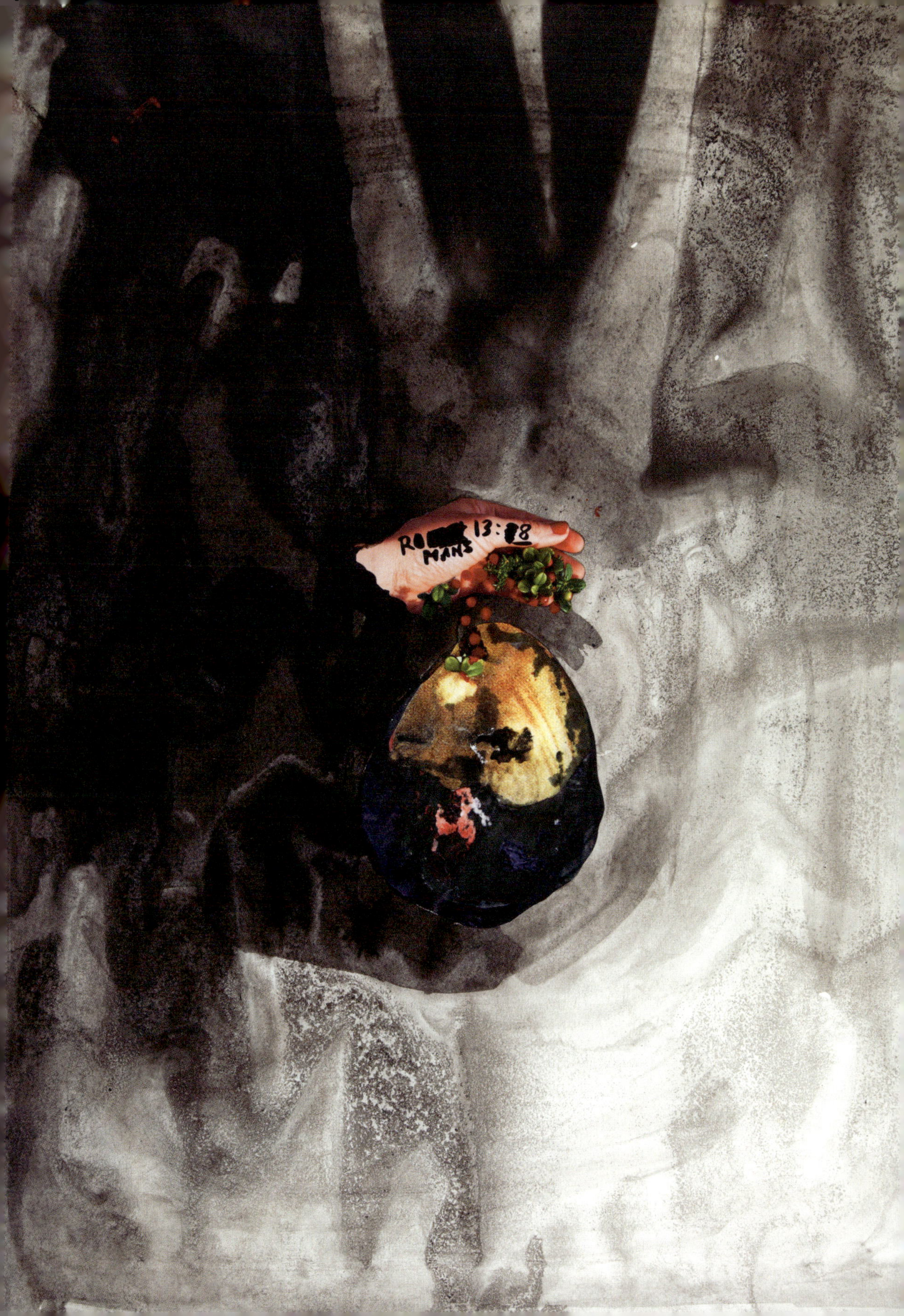
ROMANS 13:08

SEEING
A
RUTABAGA
IN THE
SUPERMARKET
MADE ME
CRY

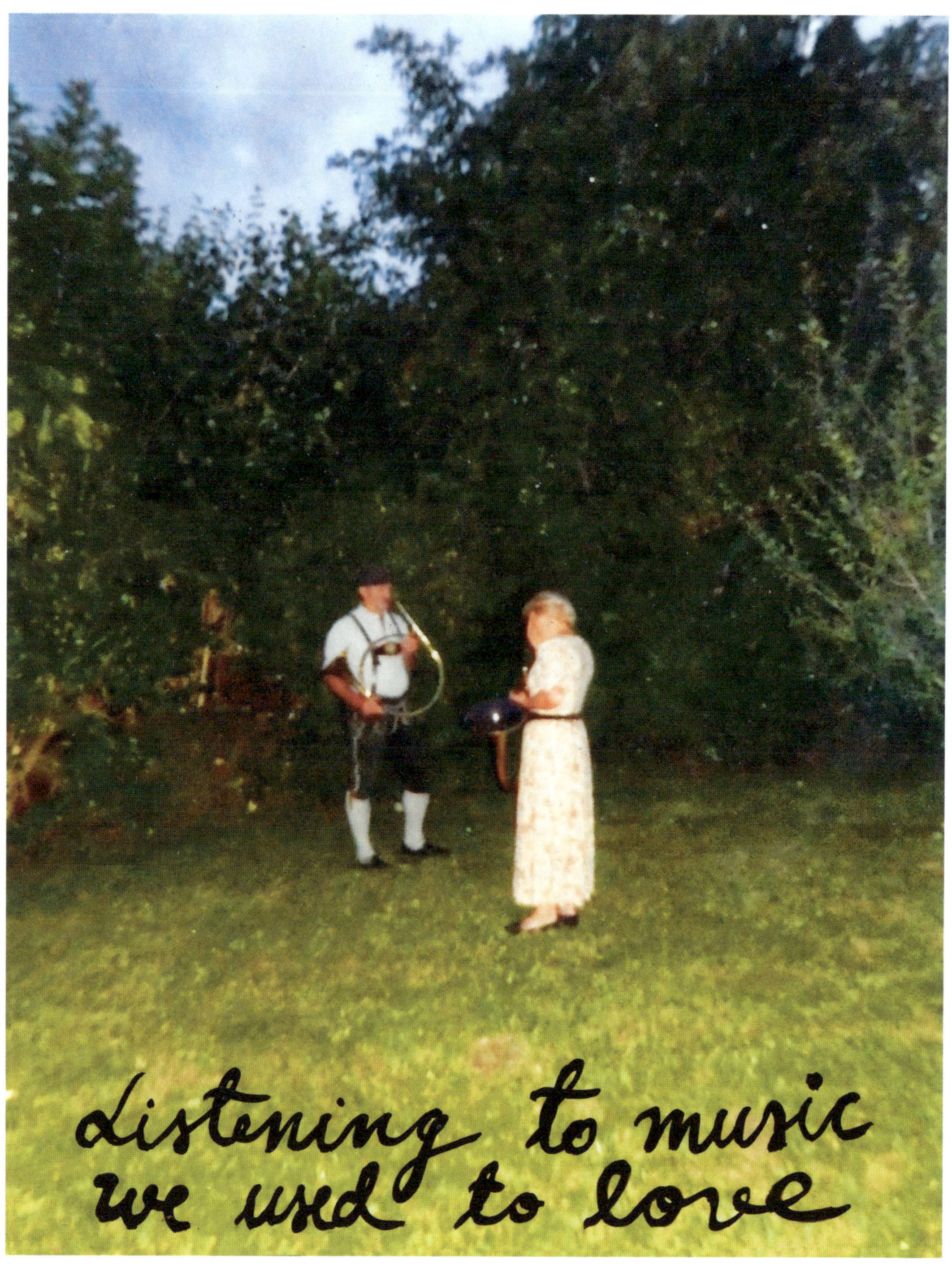
listening to music
we used to love

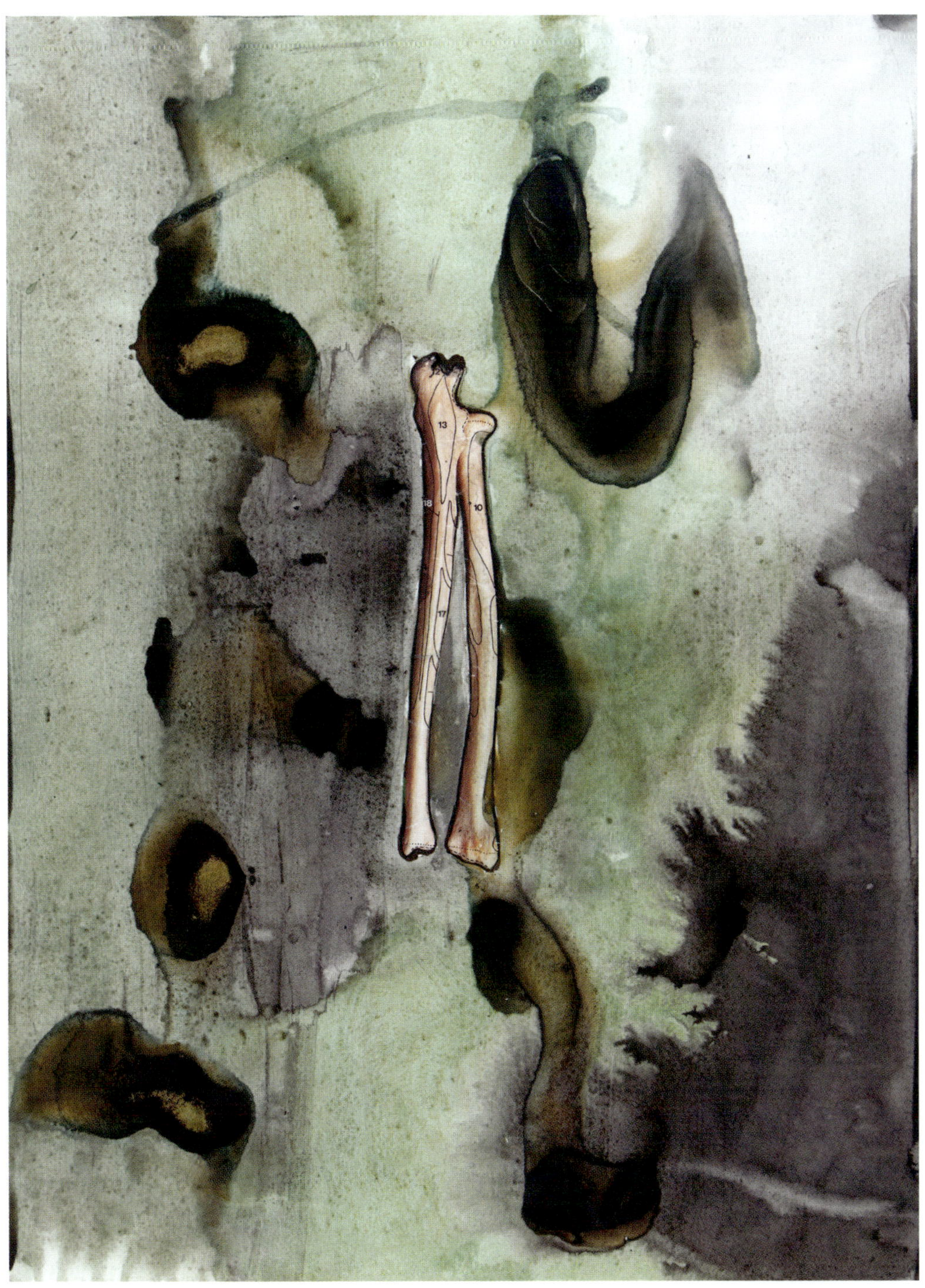

13
18
10
17

"Your Song"
sang by
Mike Skinner

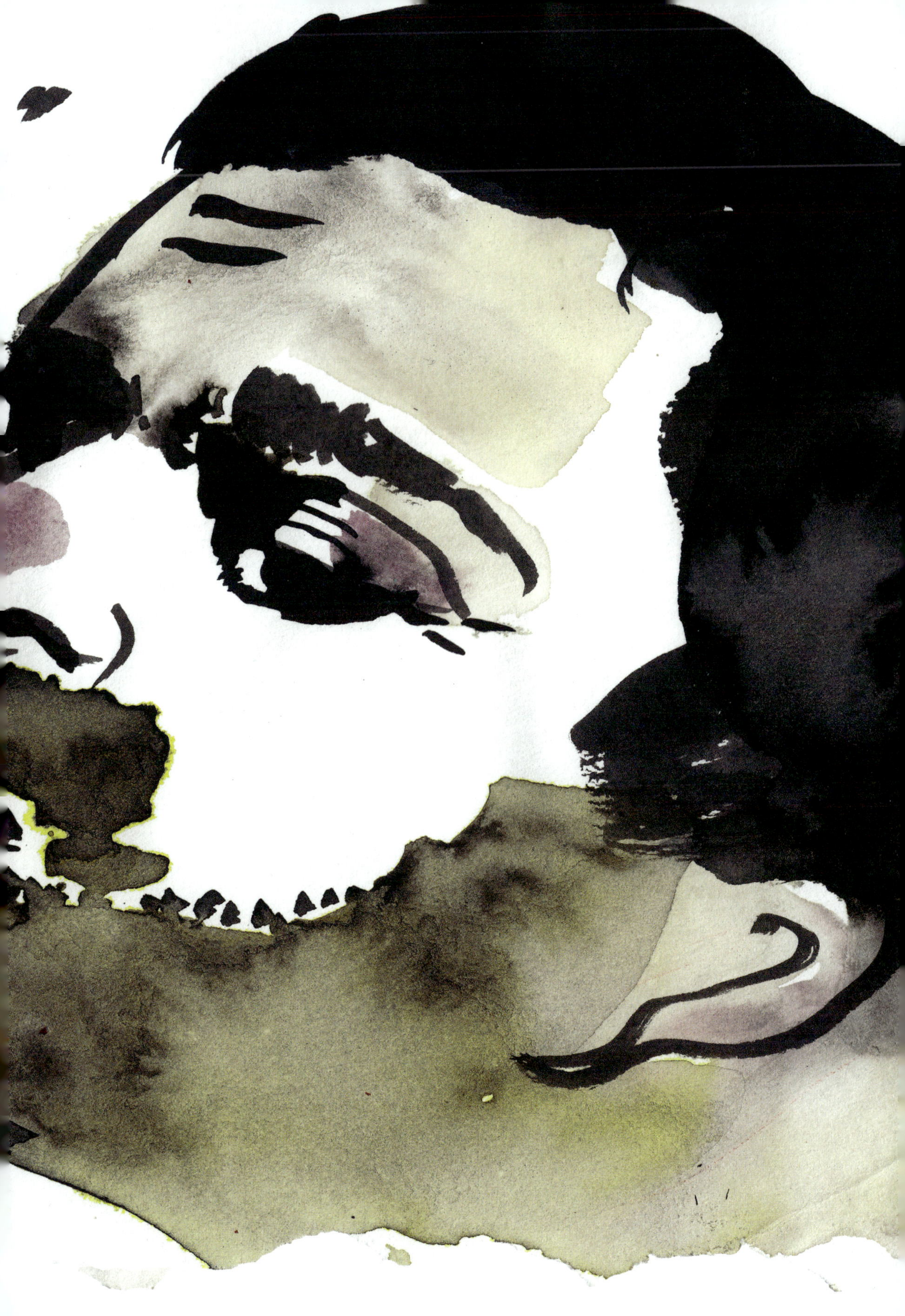

These foolish things remind
me of you:

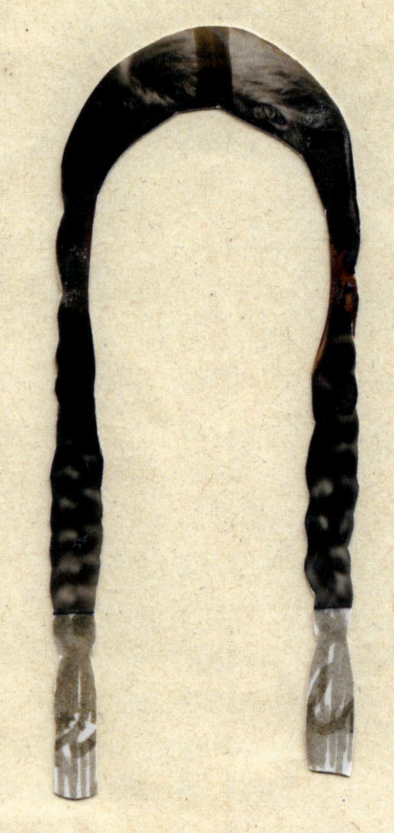

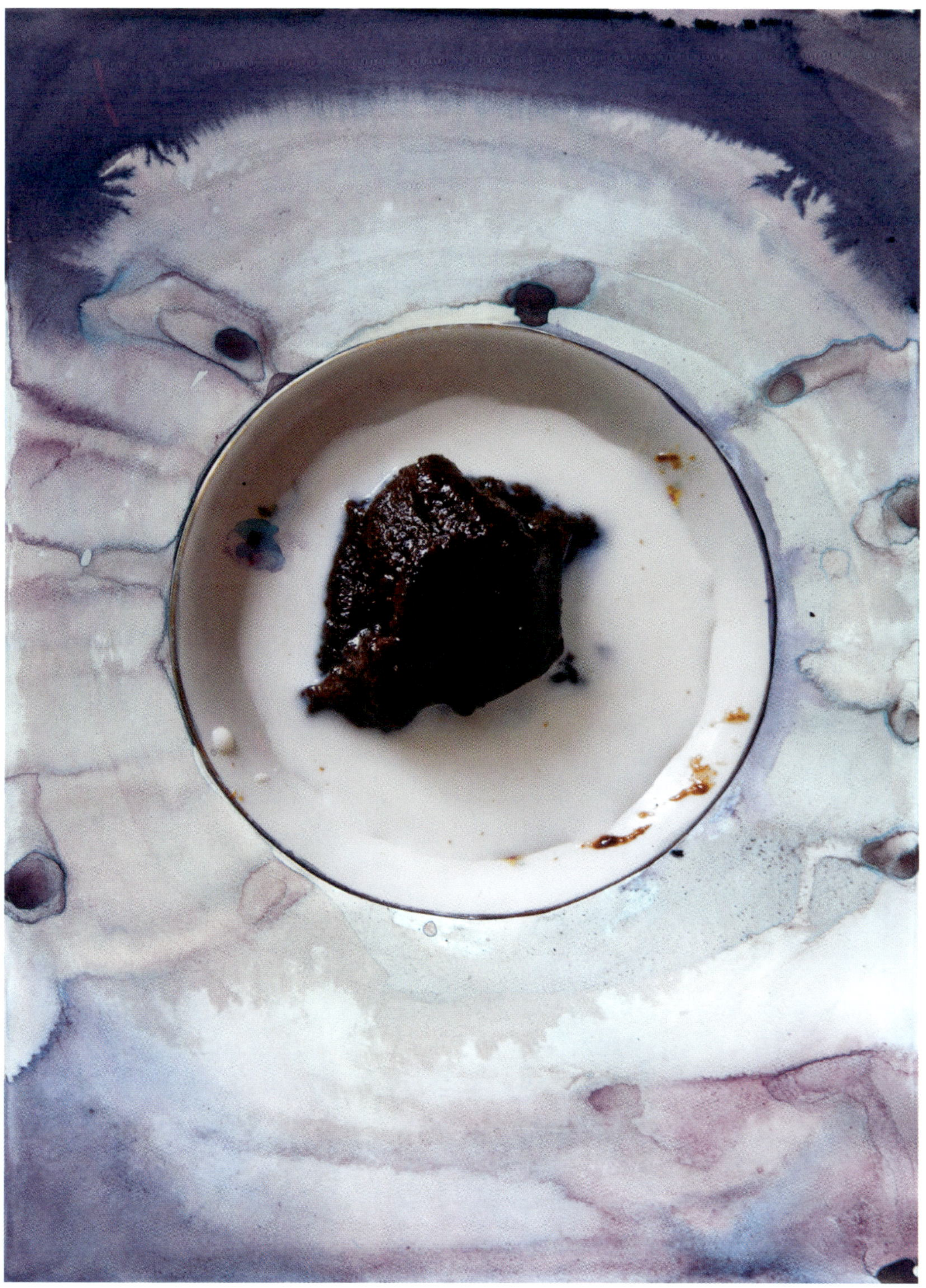

TO BE PREPARED
TO DREAM,
TO ANALYZE.
THE FLOW OF
CONVERSATION.
I'M VERTICAL
AND YOU'RE HORIZINTAL
BEFORE THE WINDOW.
IT'S SO REASSURING
TO BE ABLE TO DISCUSS
EVERYTHING WITH YOU
IT'S HARD TO SLEEP.

MOMENTS
WHEN I CAN
SPEAK
REMIND ME
OF SANNA

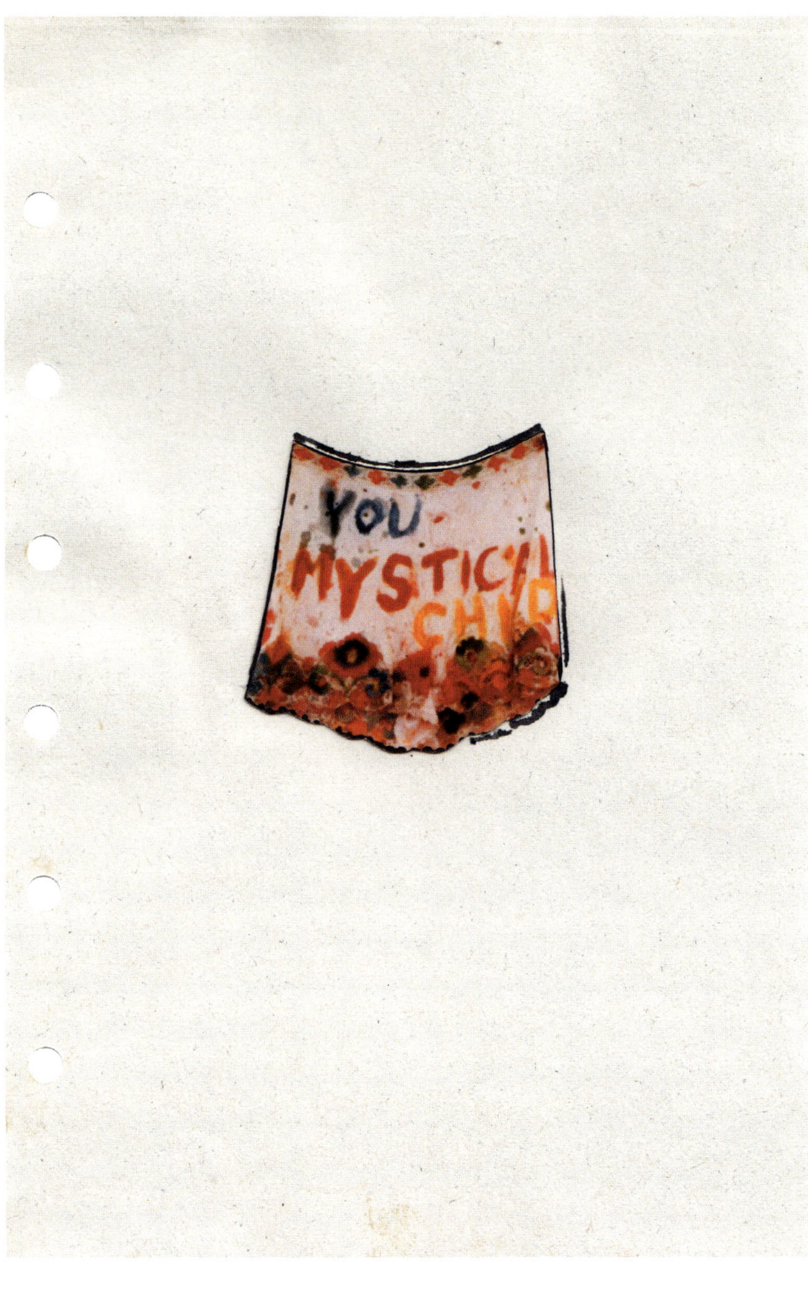
YOU
MYSTICAL
CHILD

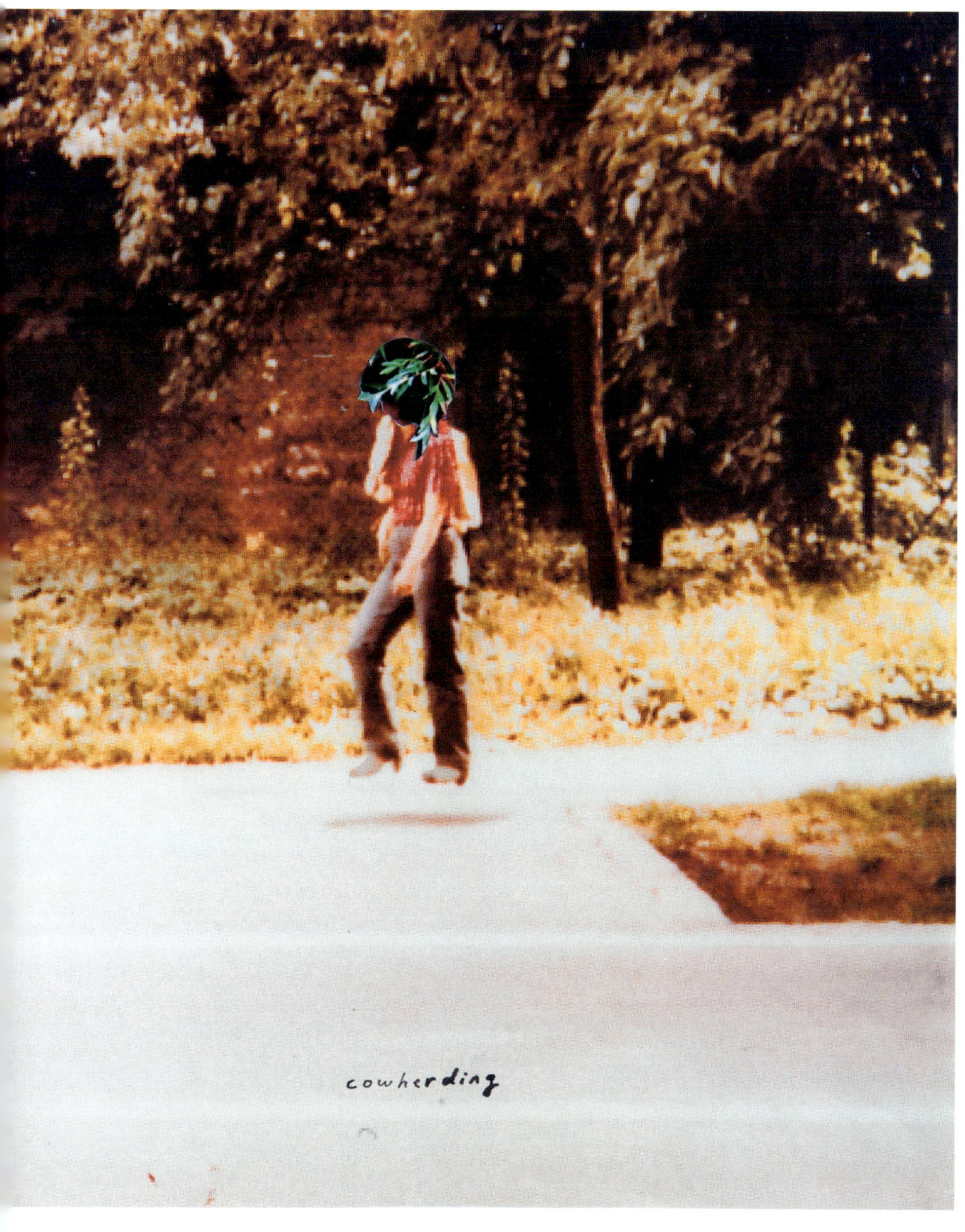

cowherding

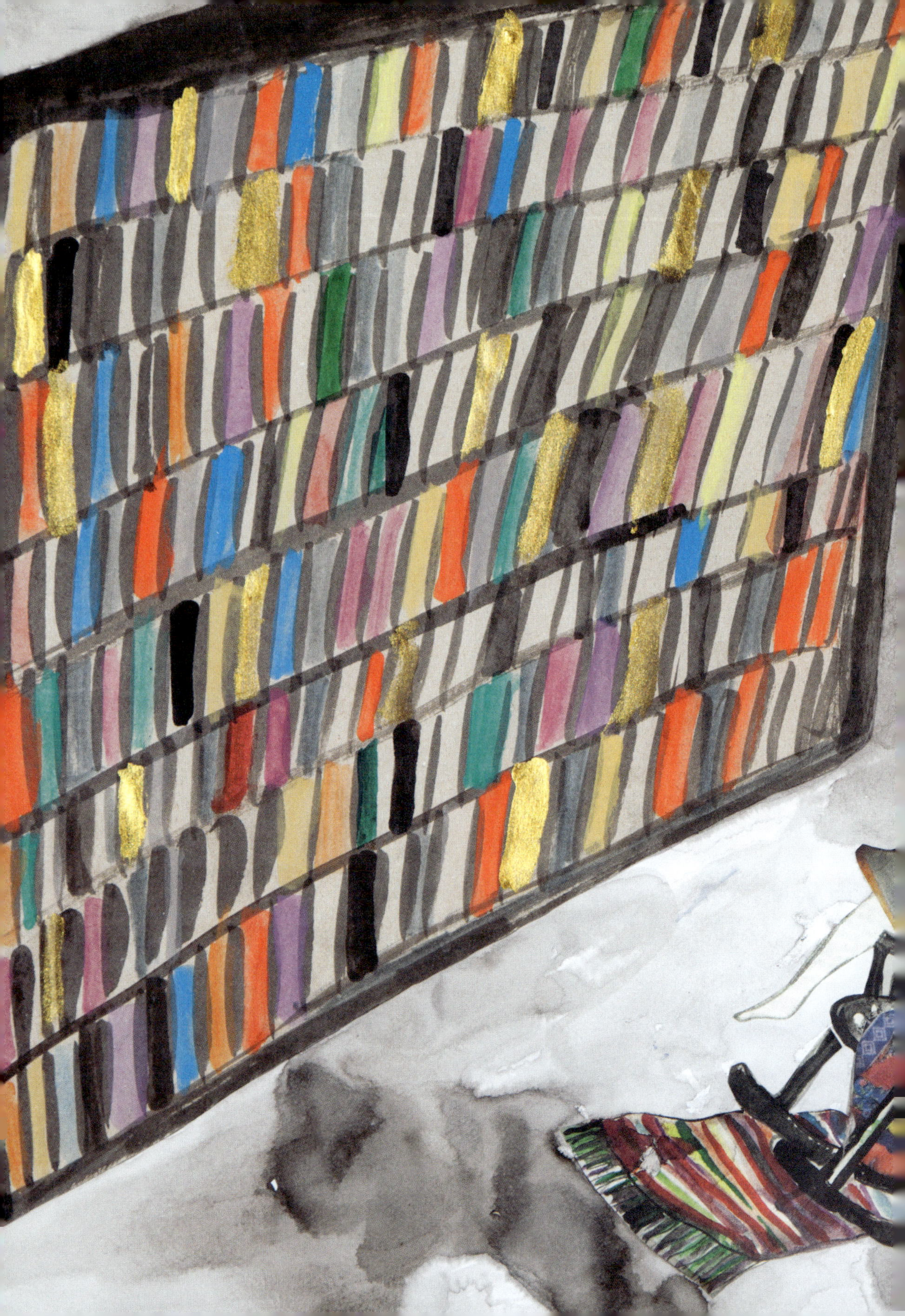

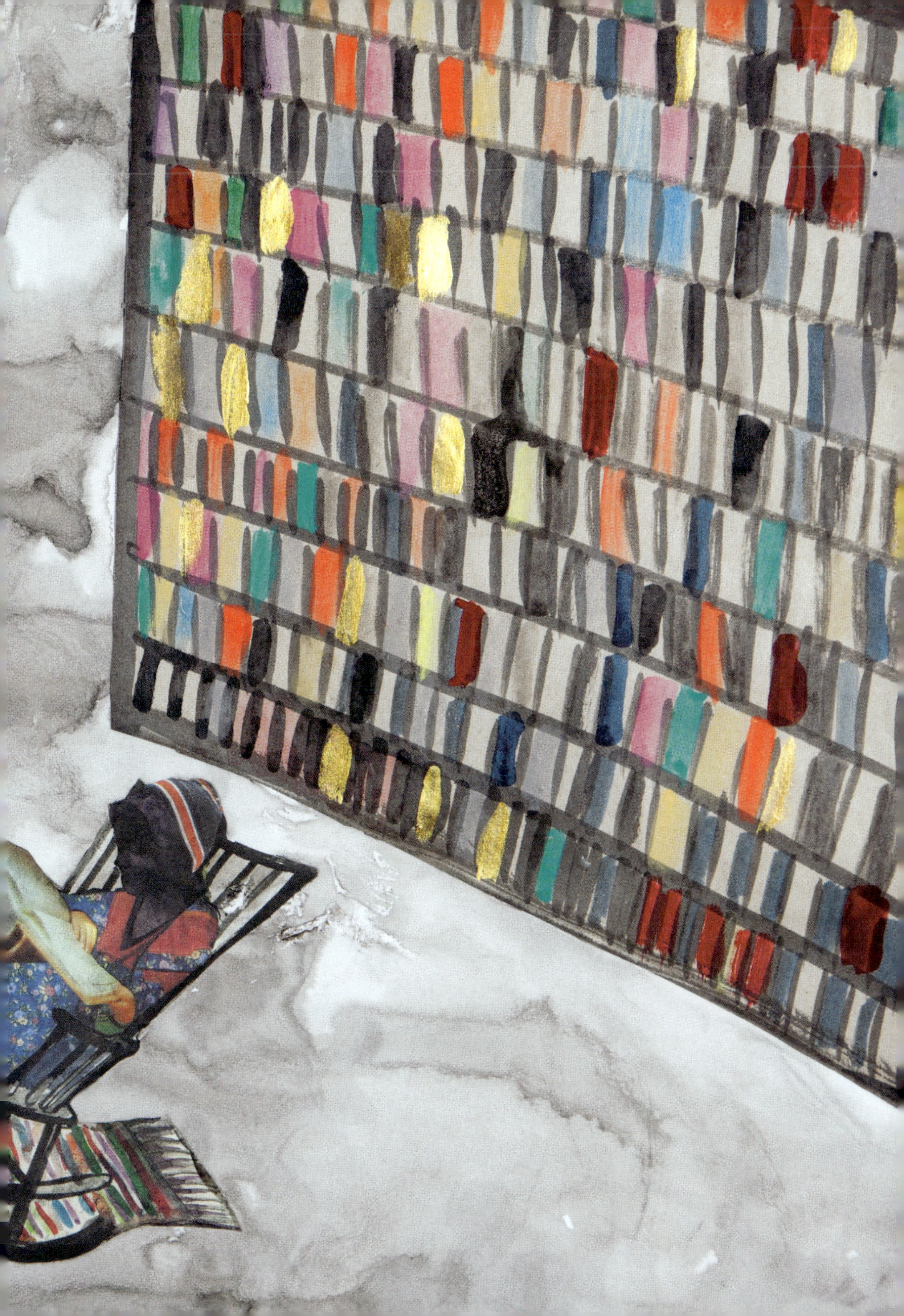

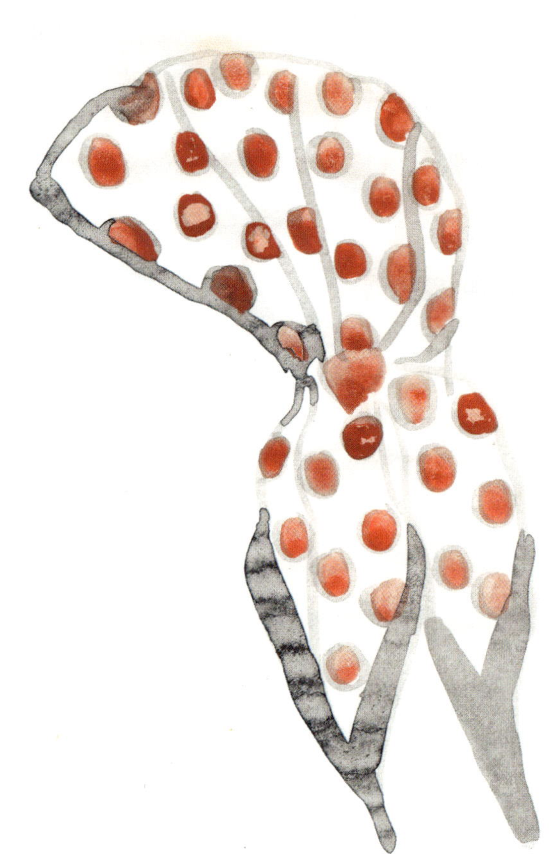

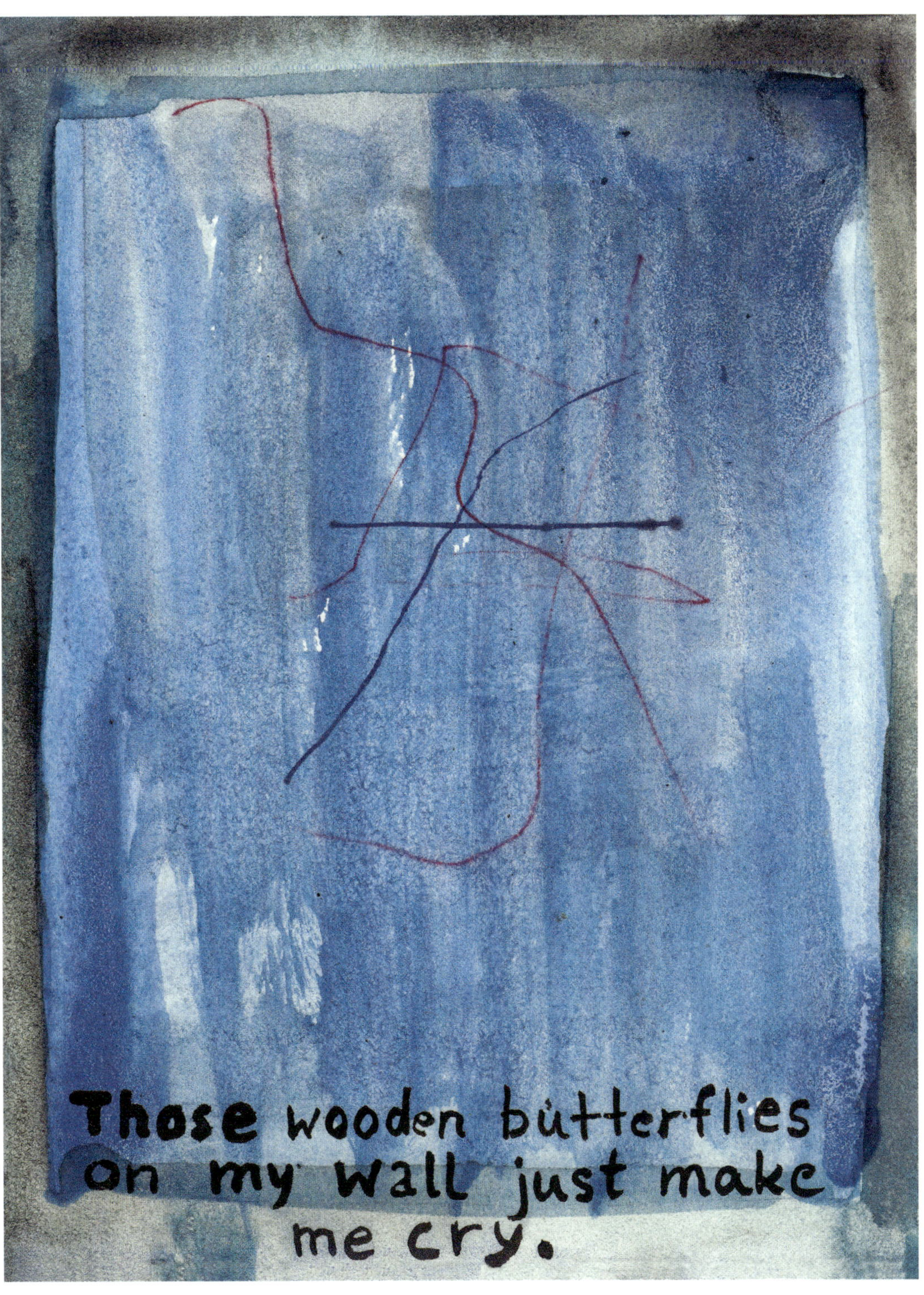
Those wooden butterflies
on my wall just make
me cry.

The taste of nettles reminds me of Aimo. (He hanged himself in Pispala shortly before the house where we were all living was torn down. They built a supermarket parking lot in its place.)

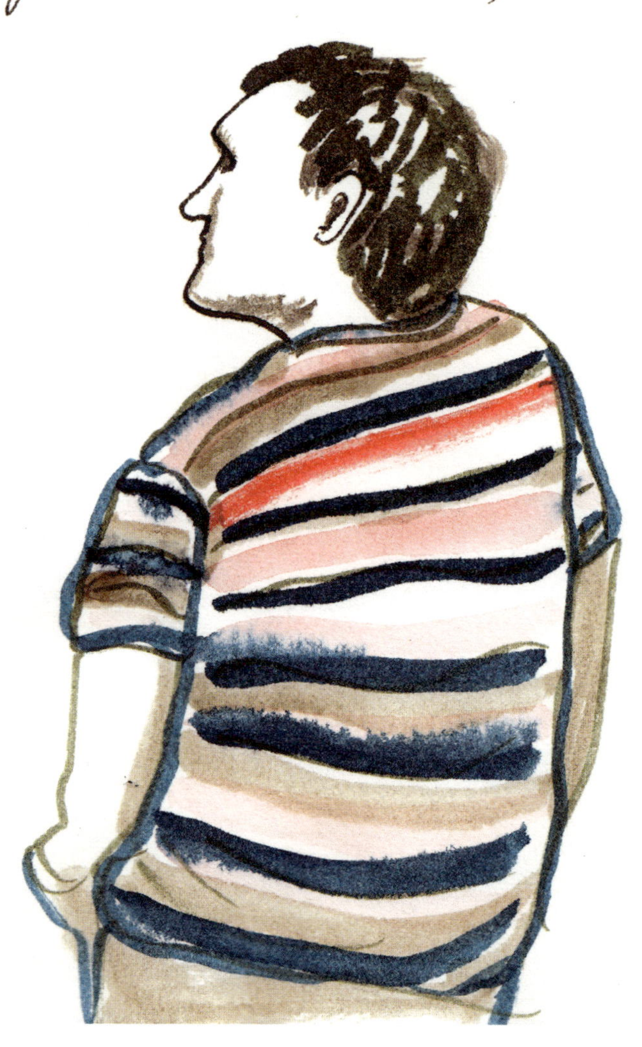

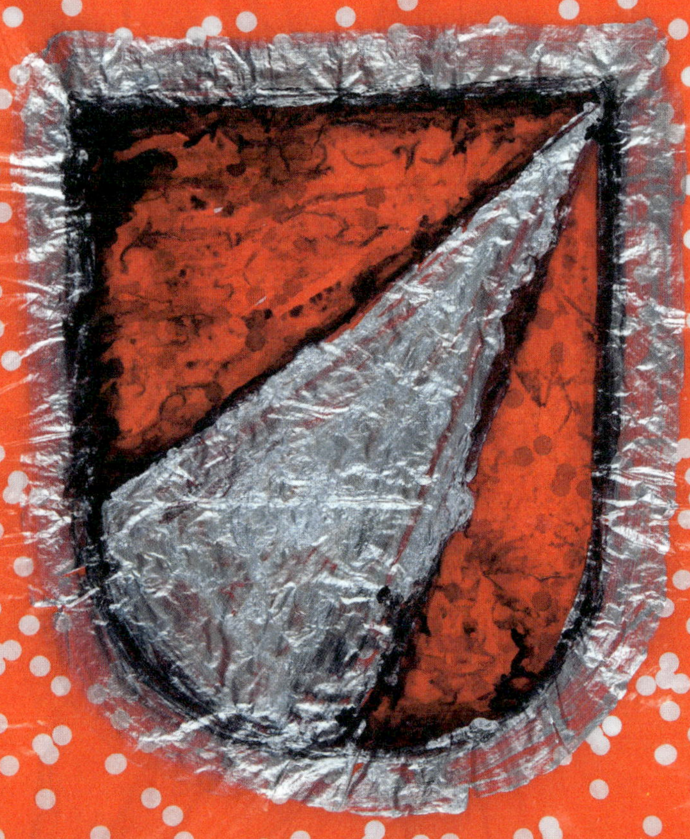

UUKUNIEMI

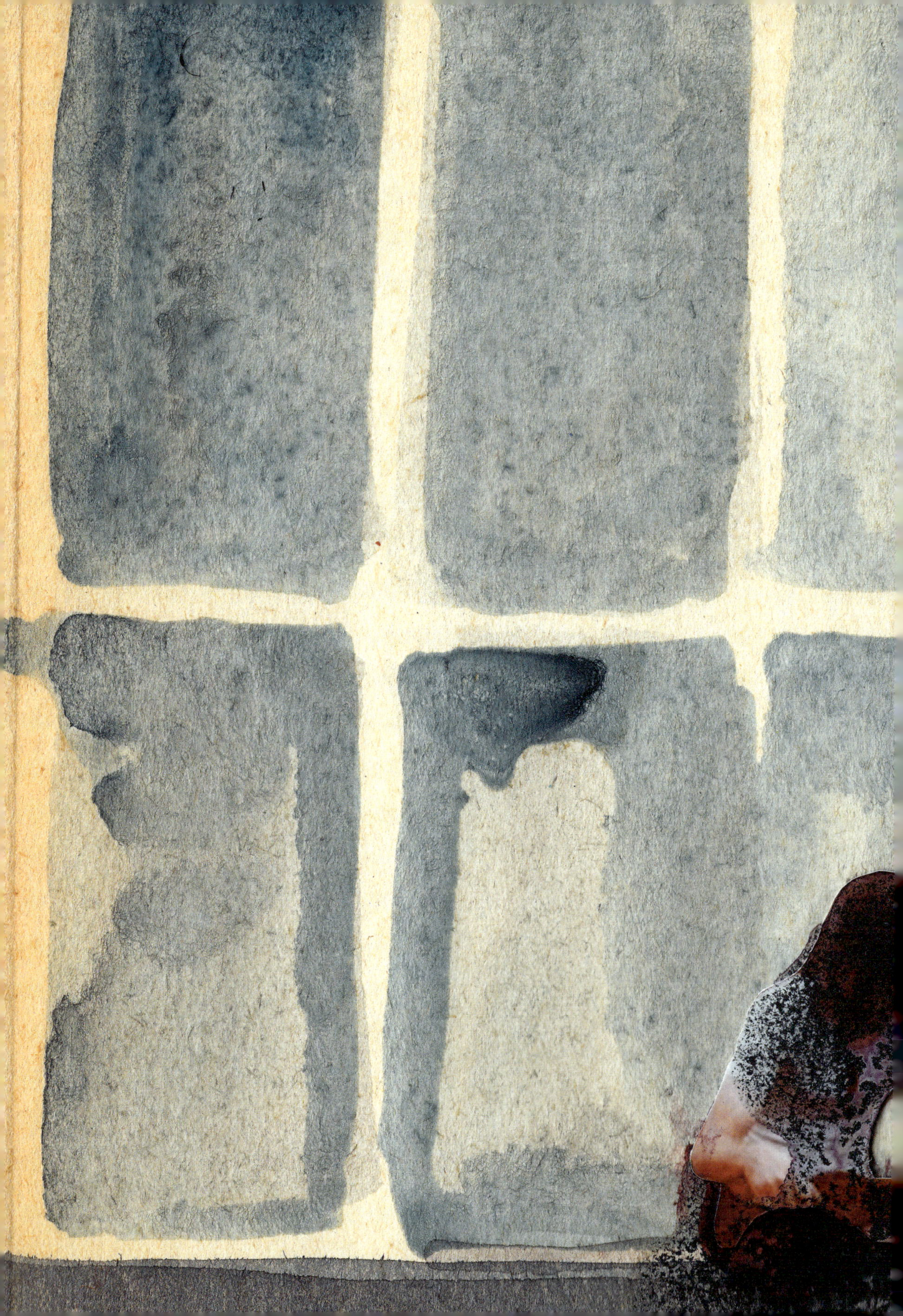

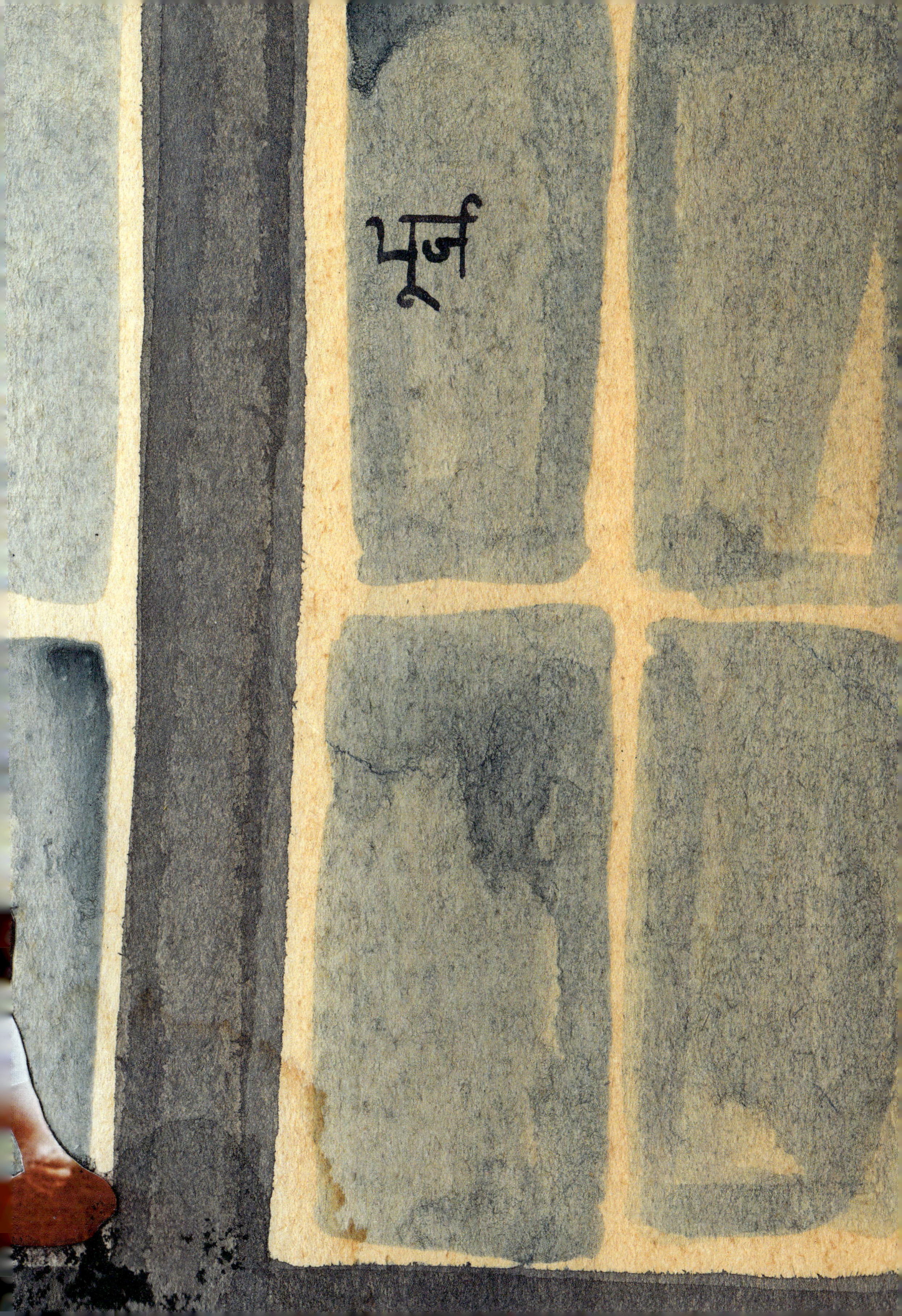
भूर्ज

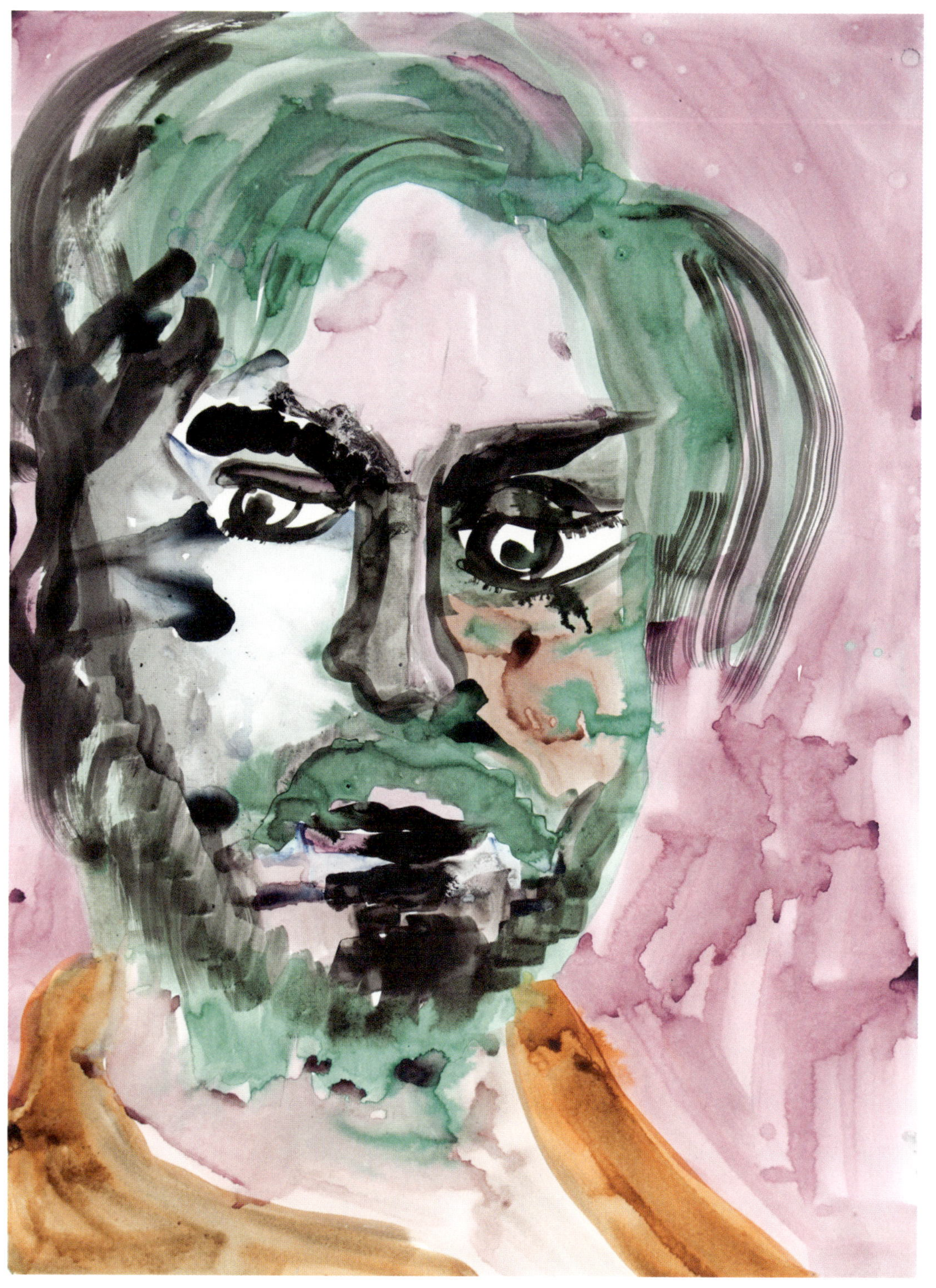

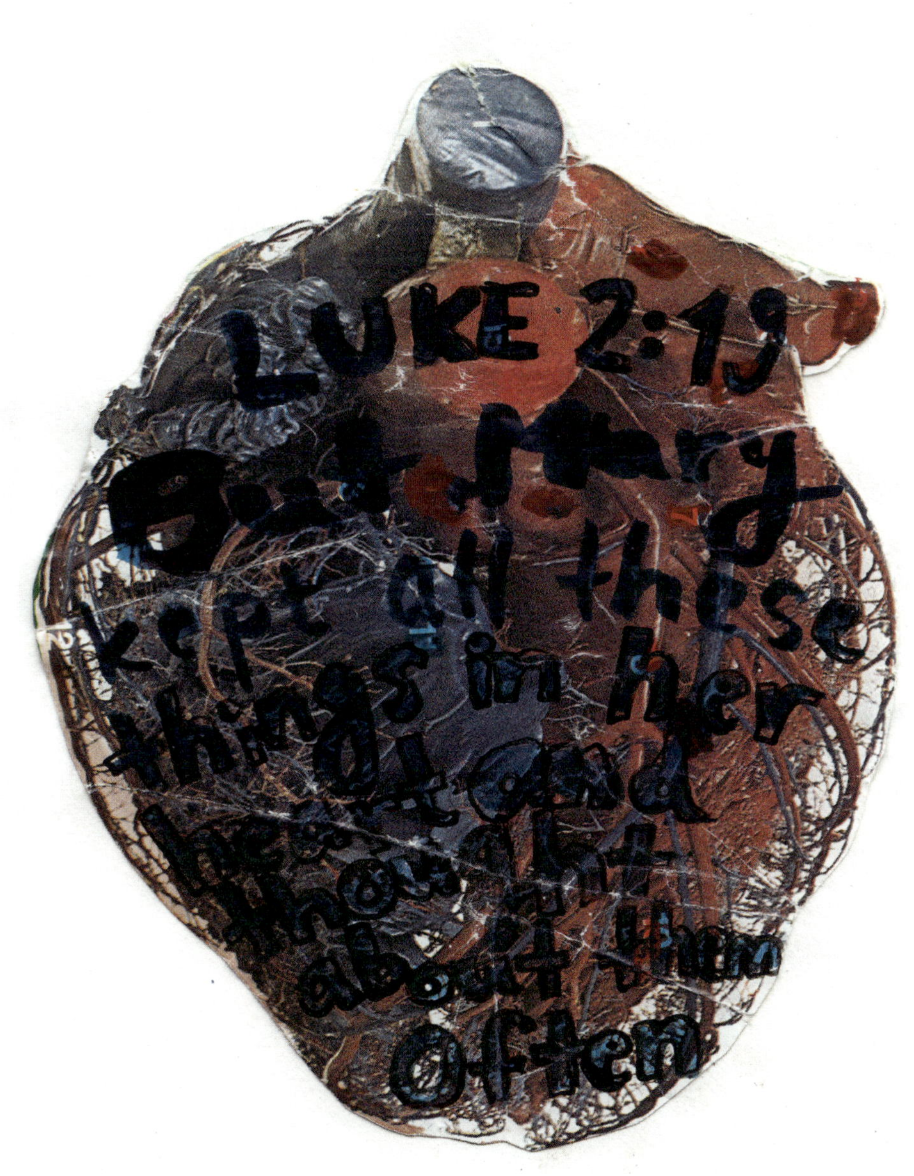

LUKE 2:19
But Mary
kept all these
things in her
heart and
thought
about them
often

CURRENT
93

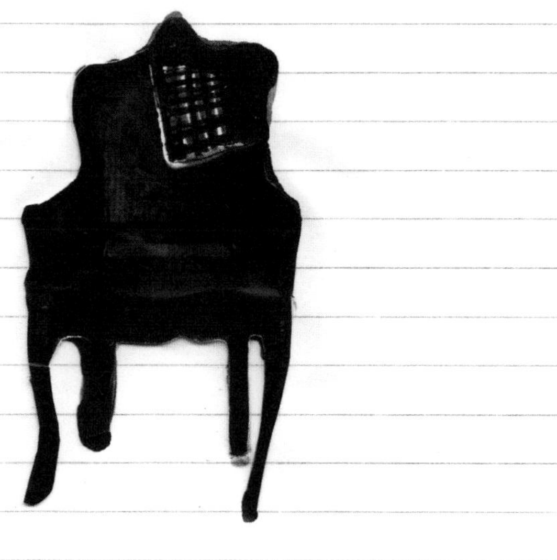

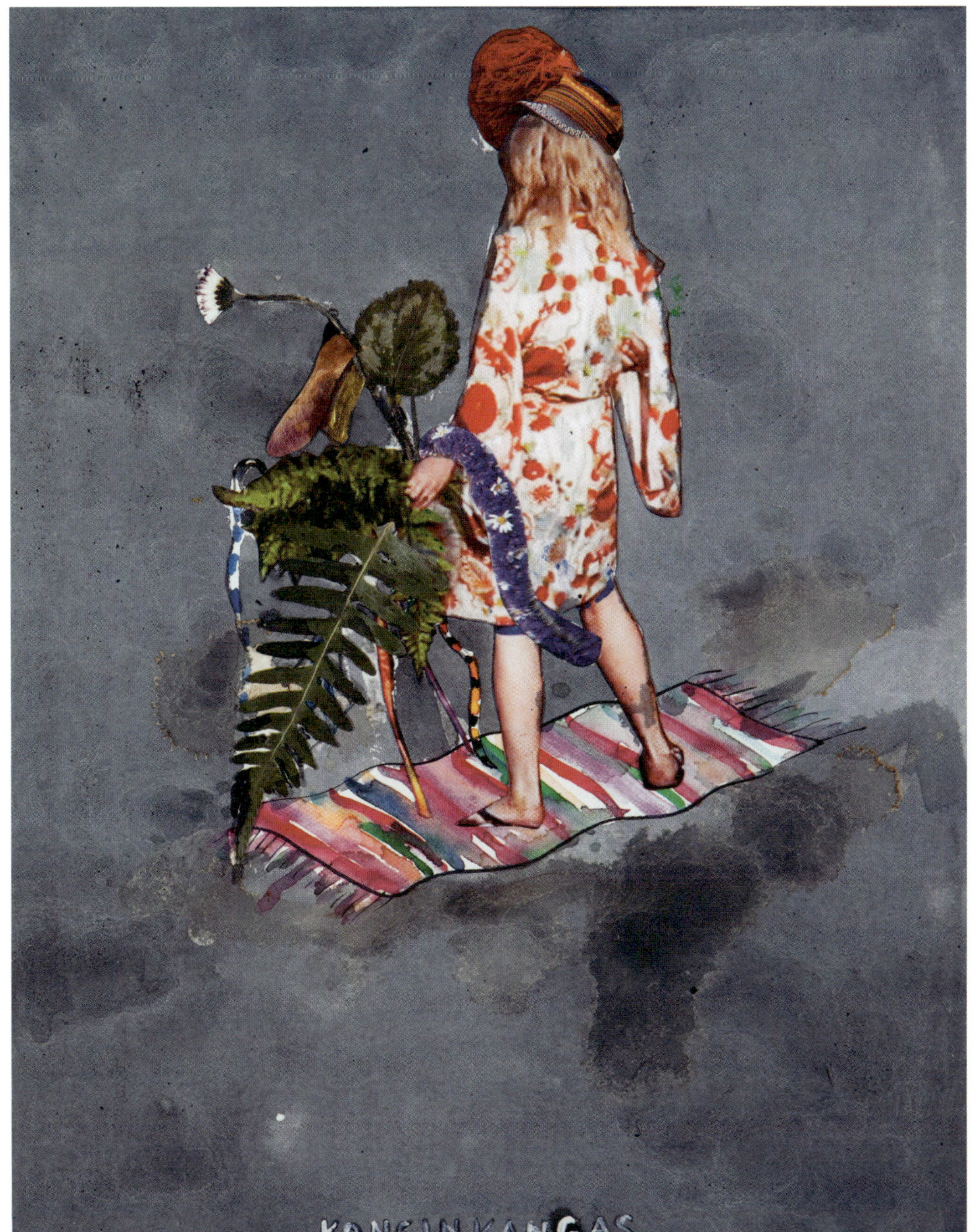
KONGINKANGAS

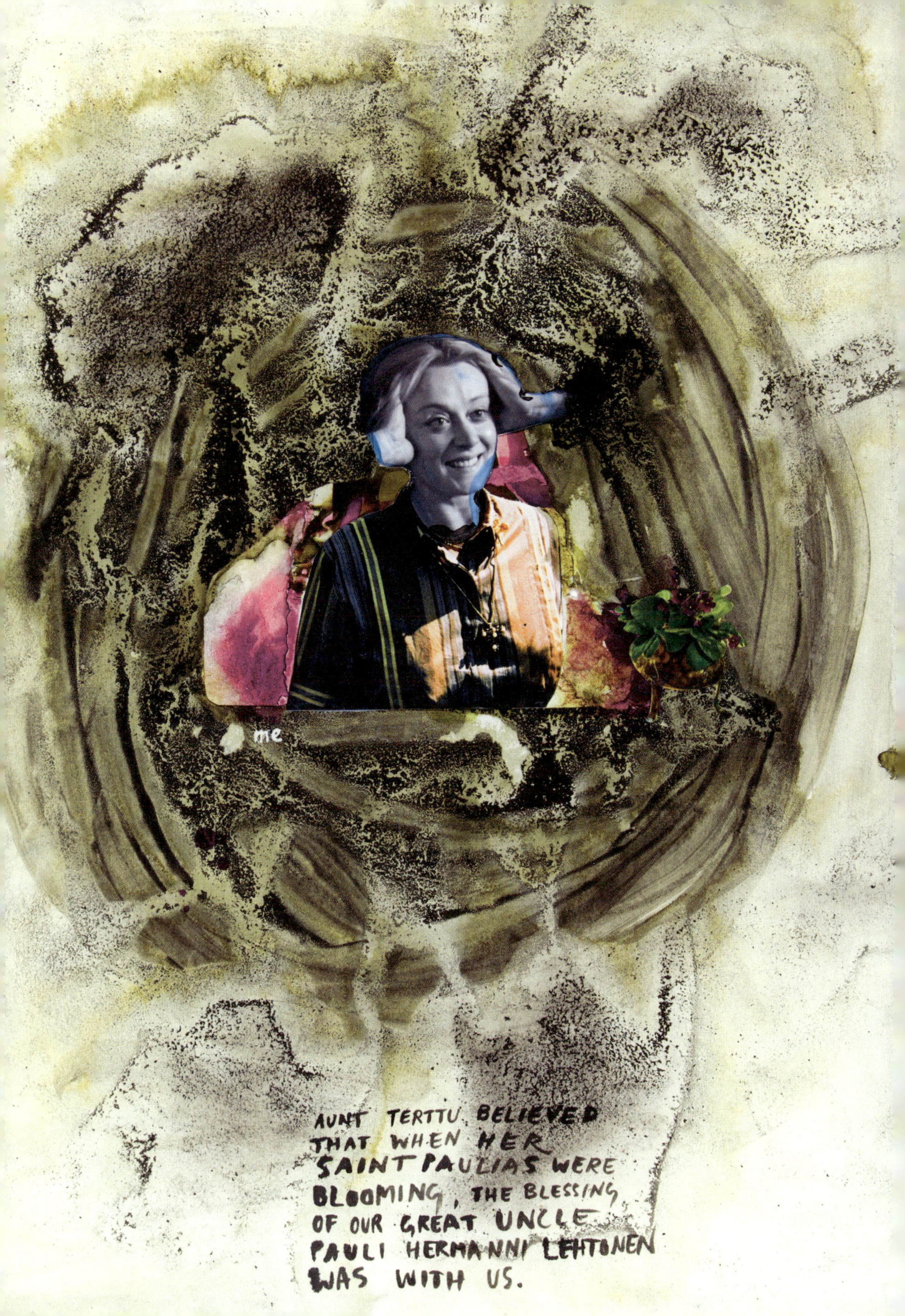

AUNT TERTTU BELIEVED
THAT WHEN HER
SAINT PAULIAS WERE
BLOOMING, THE BLESSING
OF OUR GREAT UNCLE
PAULI HERMANNI LEHTONEN
WAS WITH US.

PUFFED SLEEVES

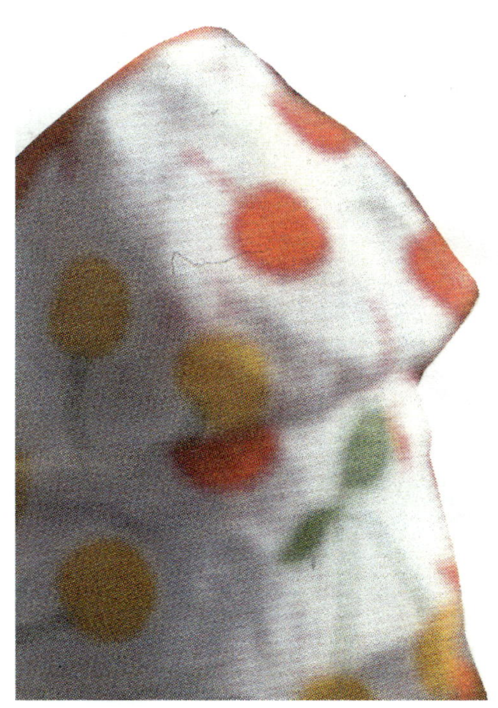

THE BOOKS OF C. CASTANEDA.

"In this astonishing and luminous work, Carlos Castaneda completes his long journey into the world of sorcery which began with his now-legendary meeting with Don Juan. This, his fourth book, describes the culmination of his extraordinary initiation into the mysteries of sorcery."

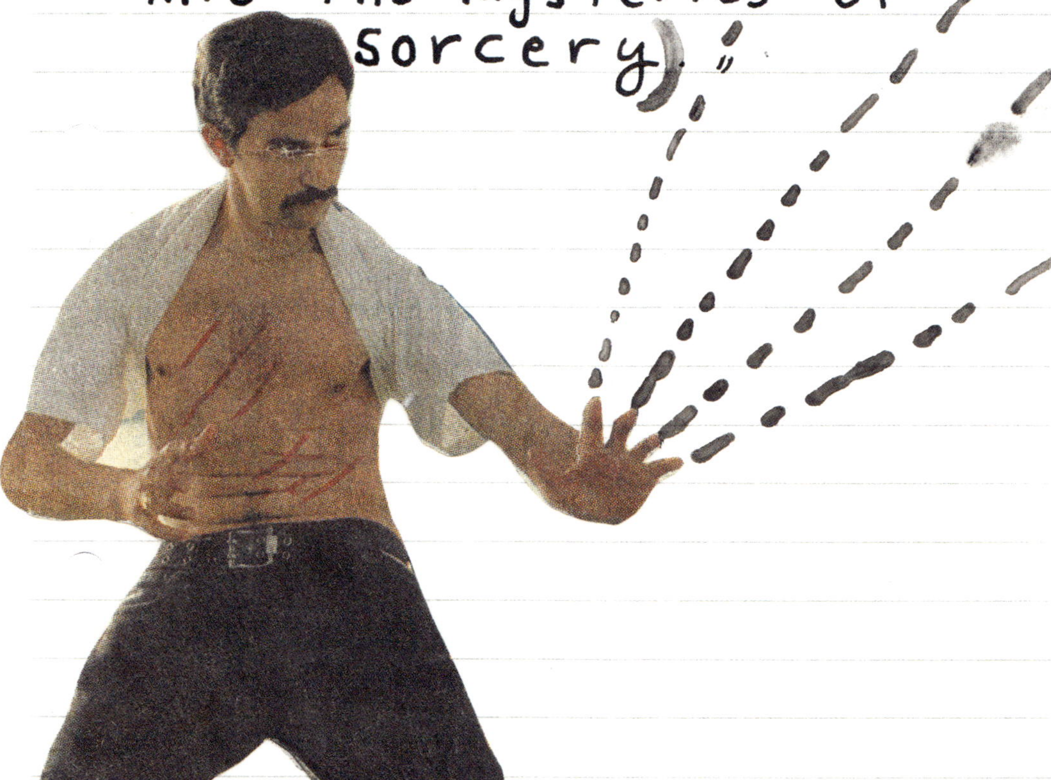

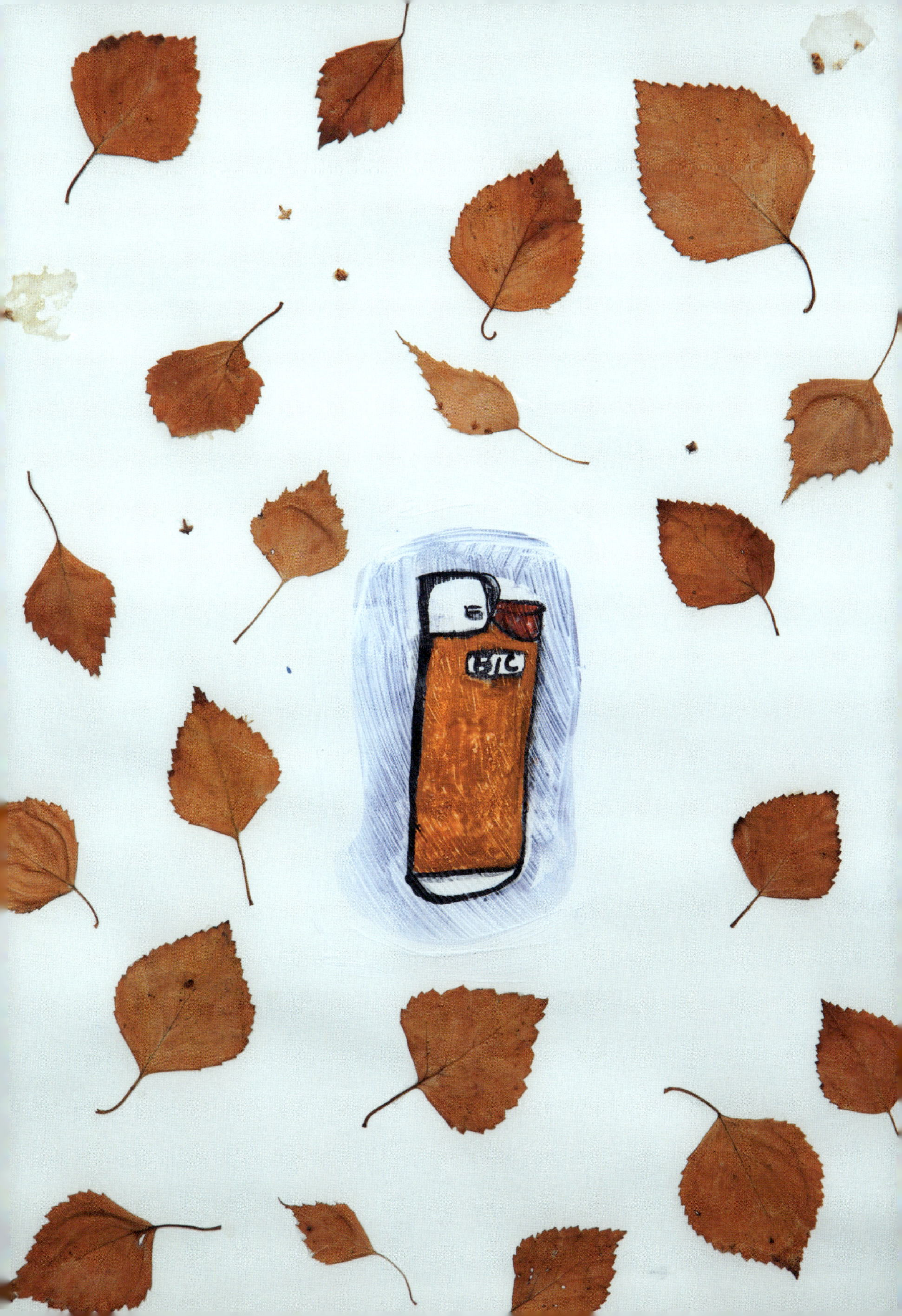
BIC

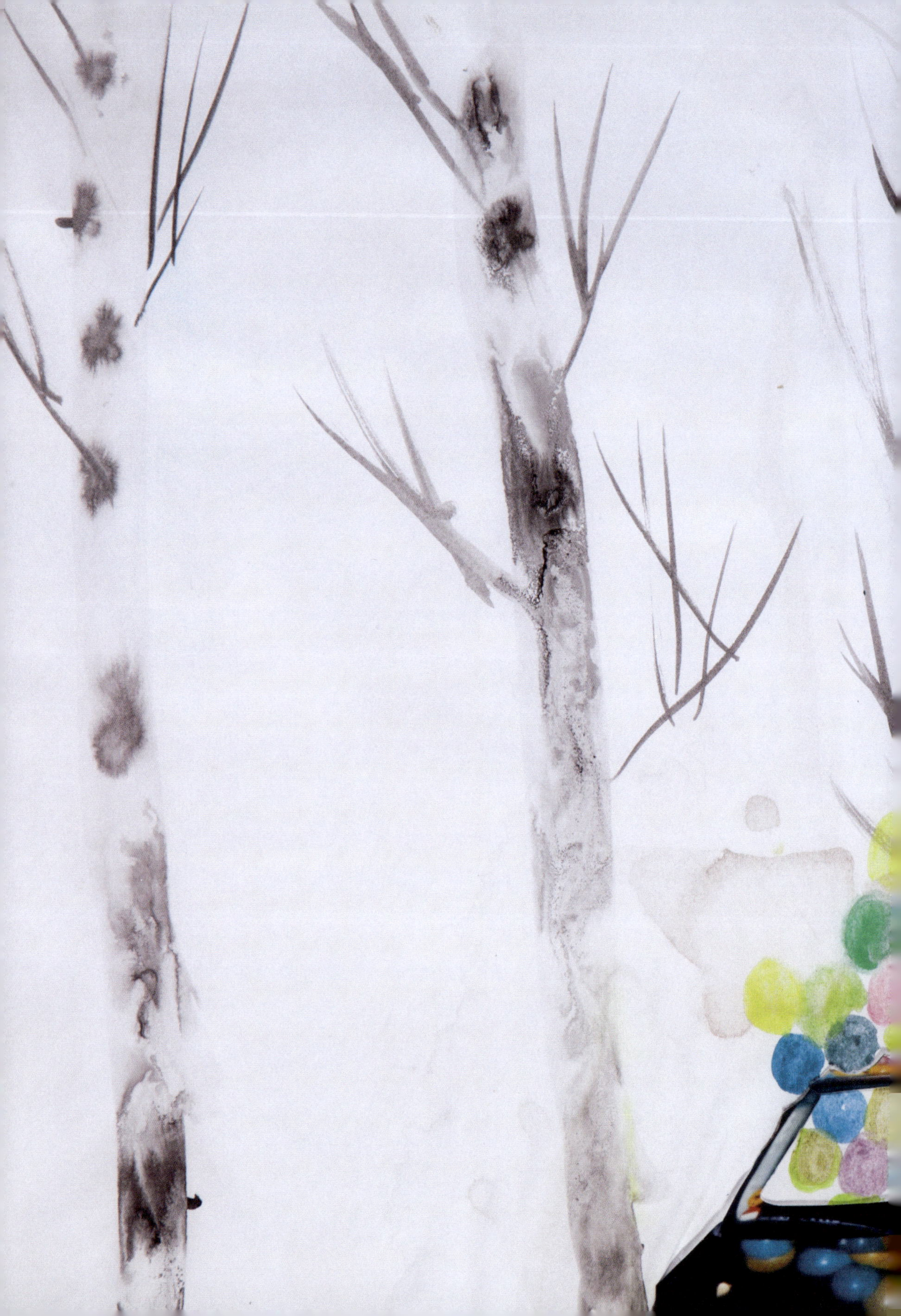

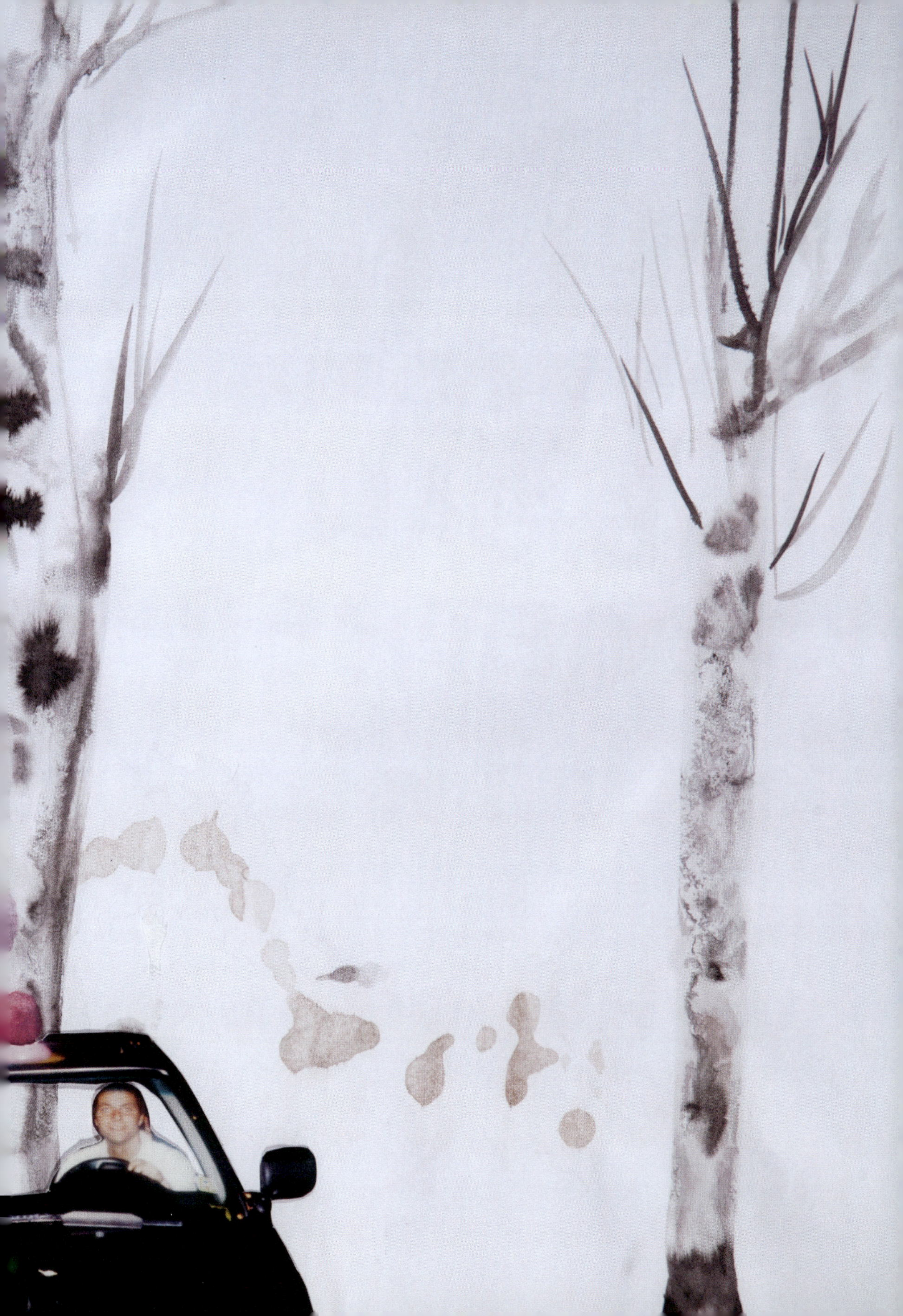

ALL THE PLACES THAT WE SAW TOGETHER, ALL THE PLACES THAT I THOUGHT WE WOULD SEE

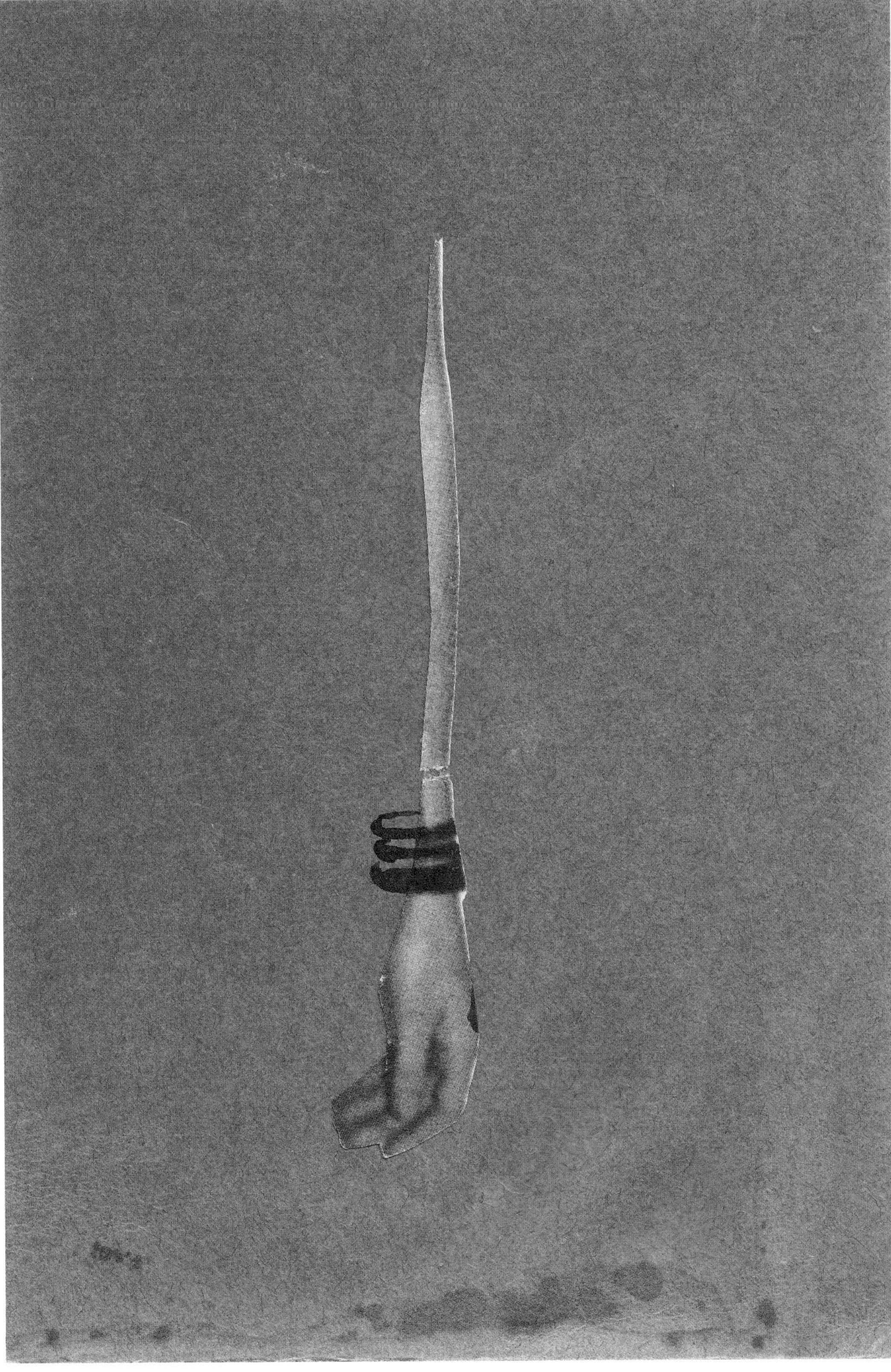

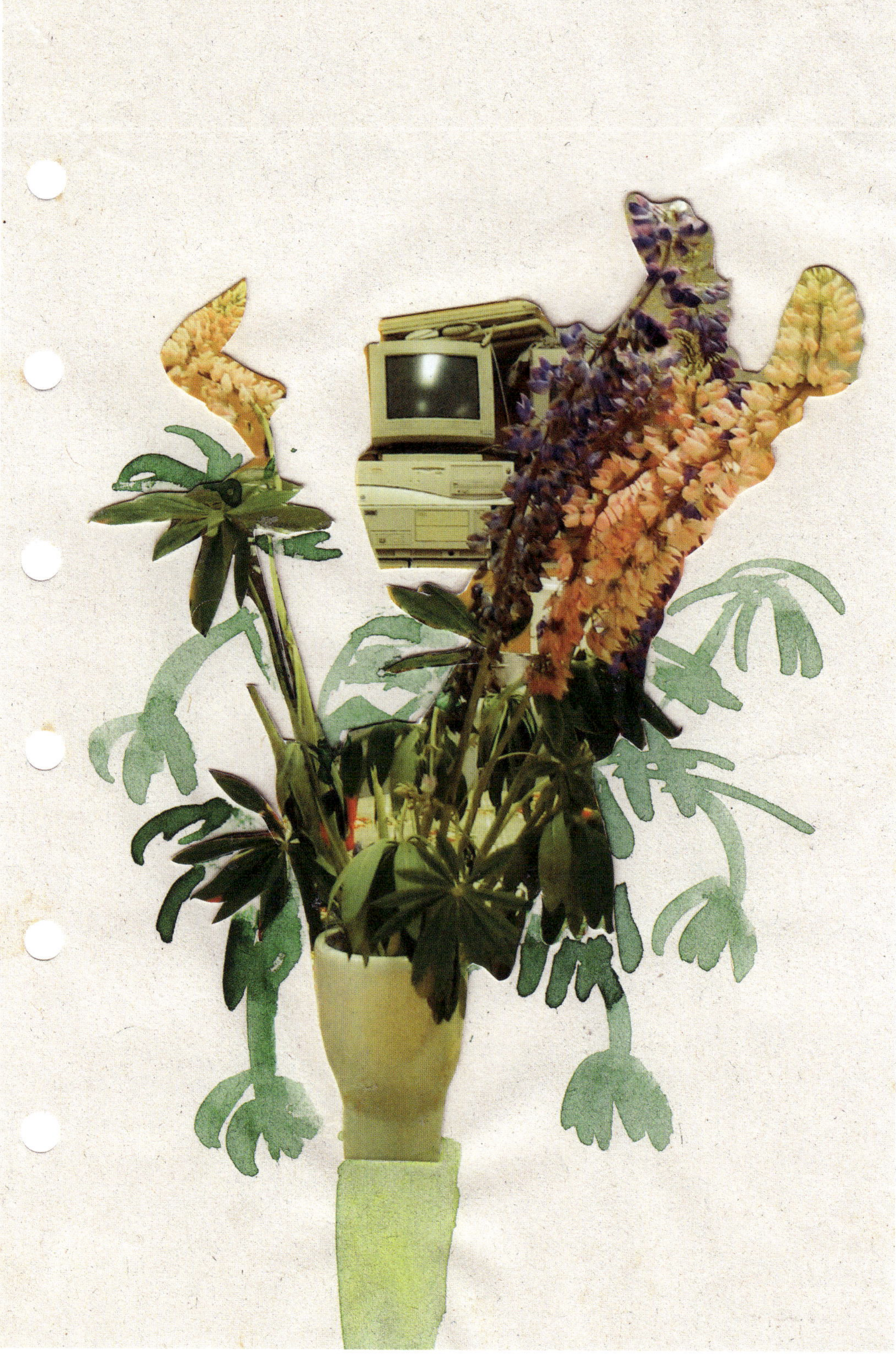

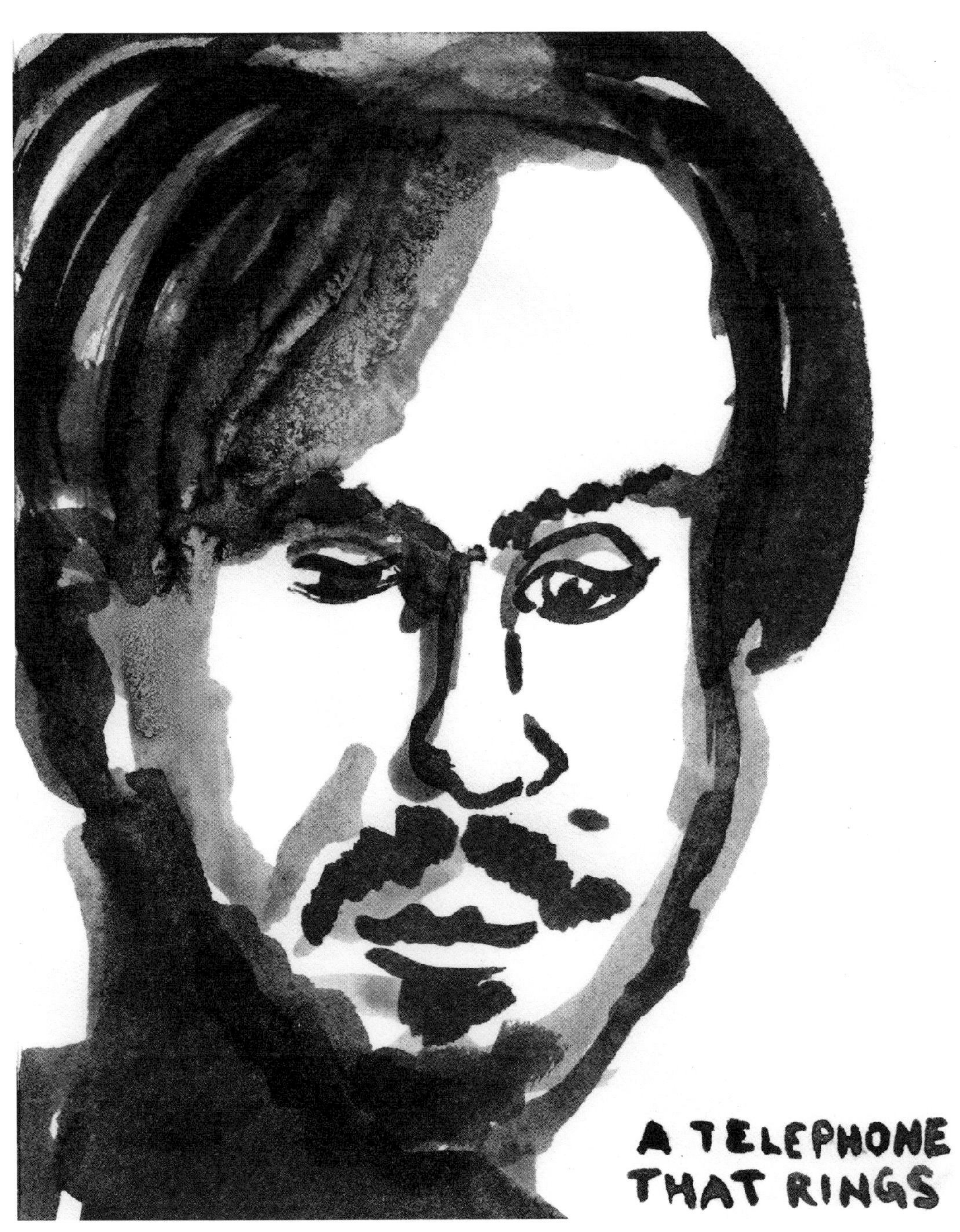

A TELEPHONE
THAT RINGS

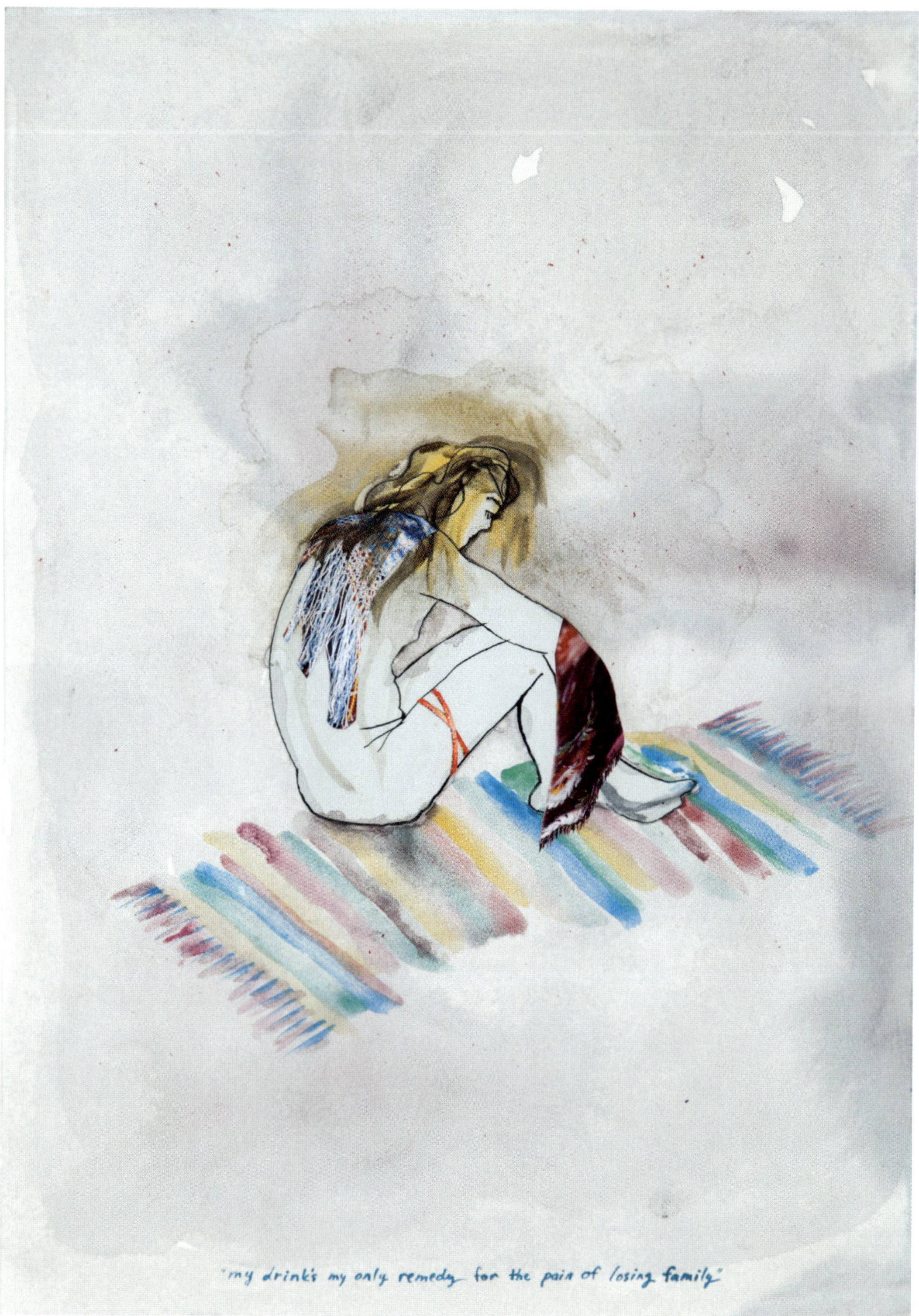

"my drink's my only remedy for the pain of losing family"

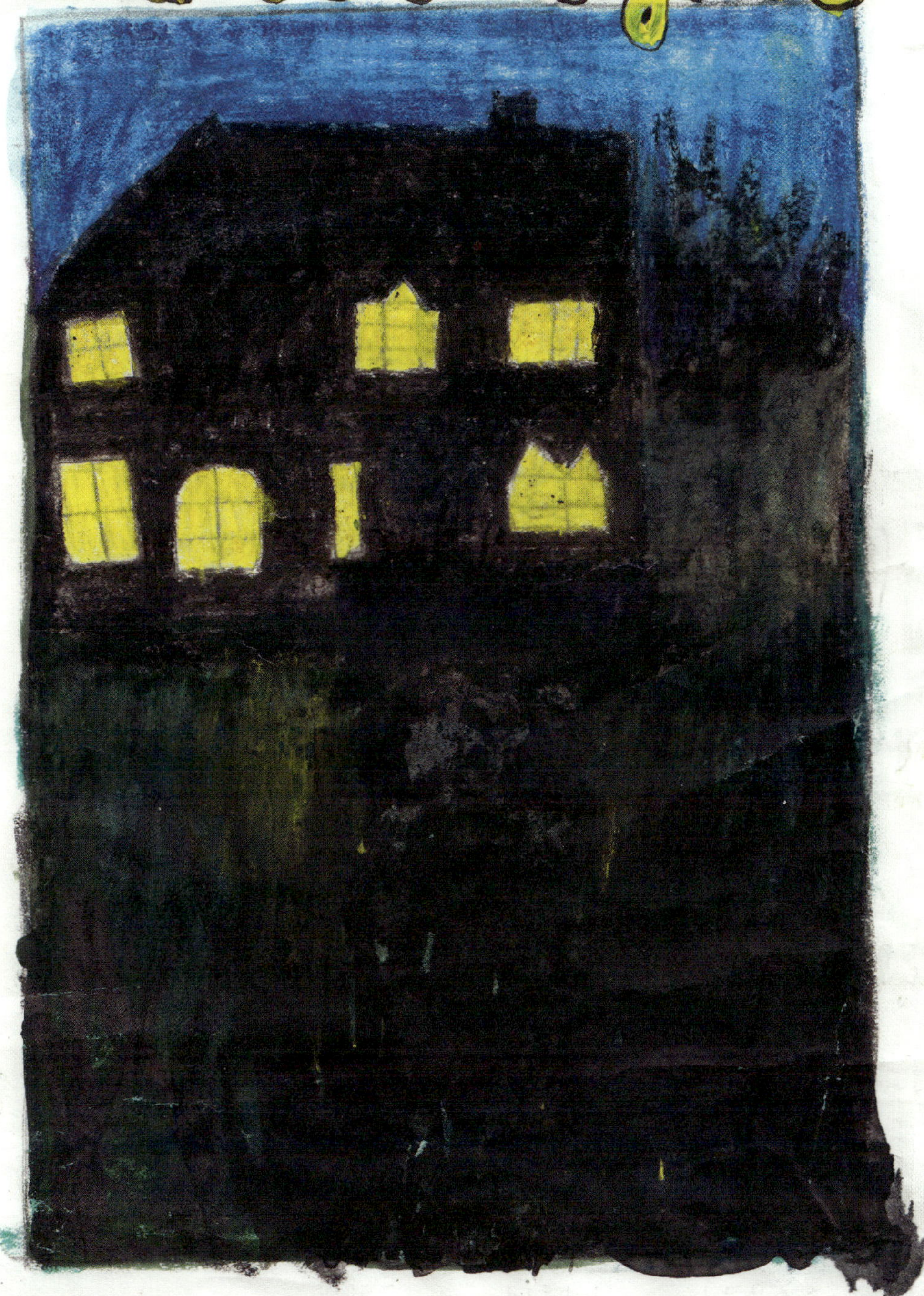

vår i Helsingfors

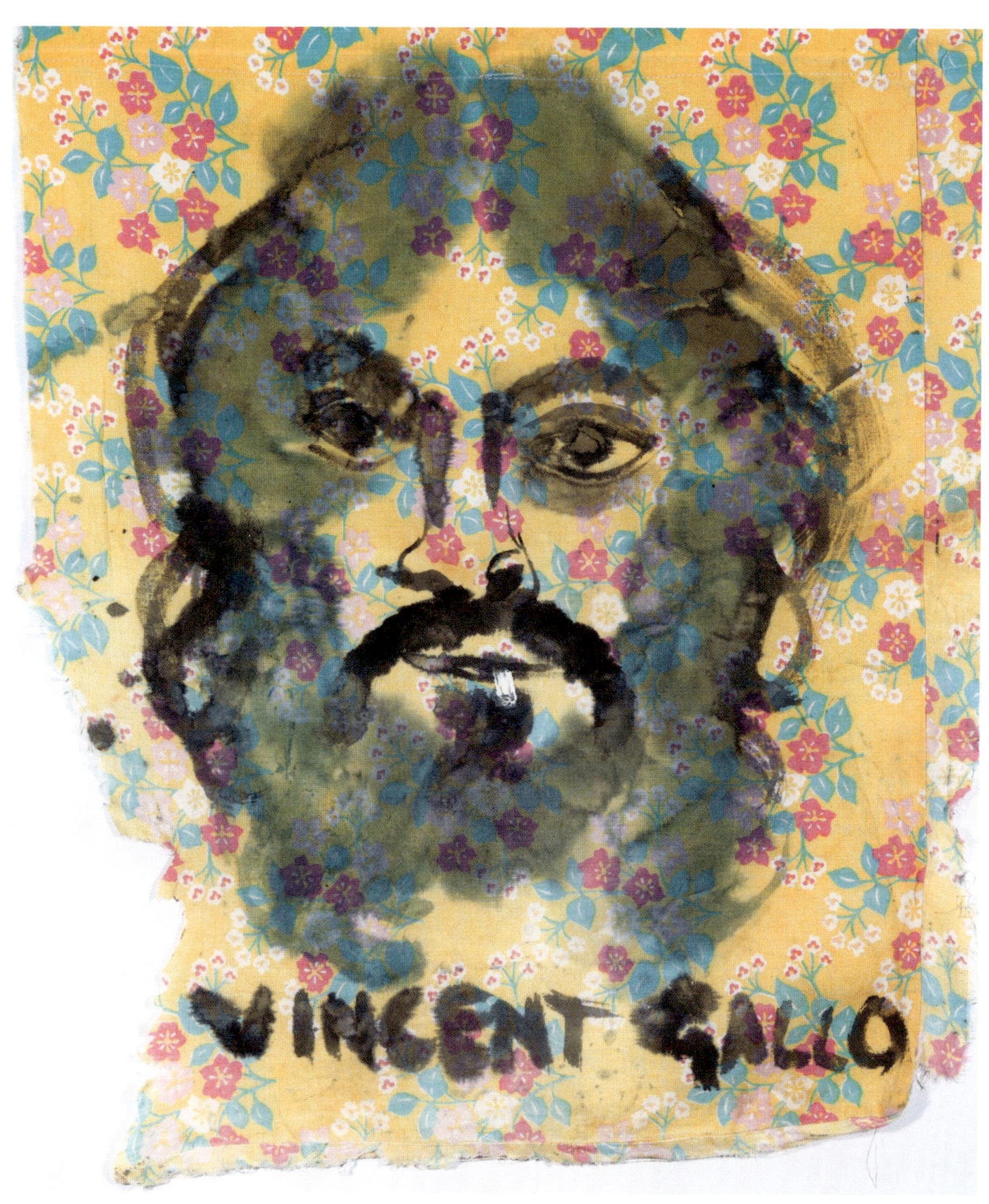

VINCENT GALLO

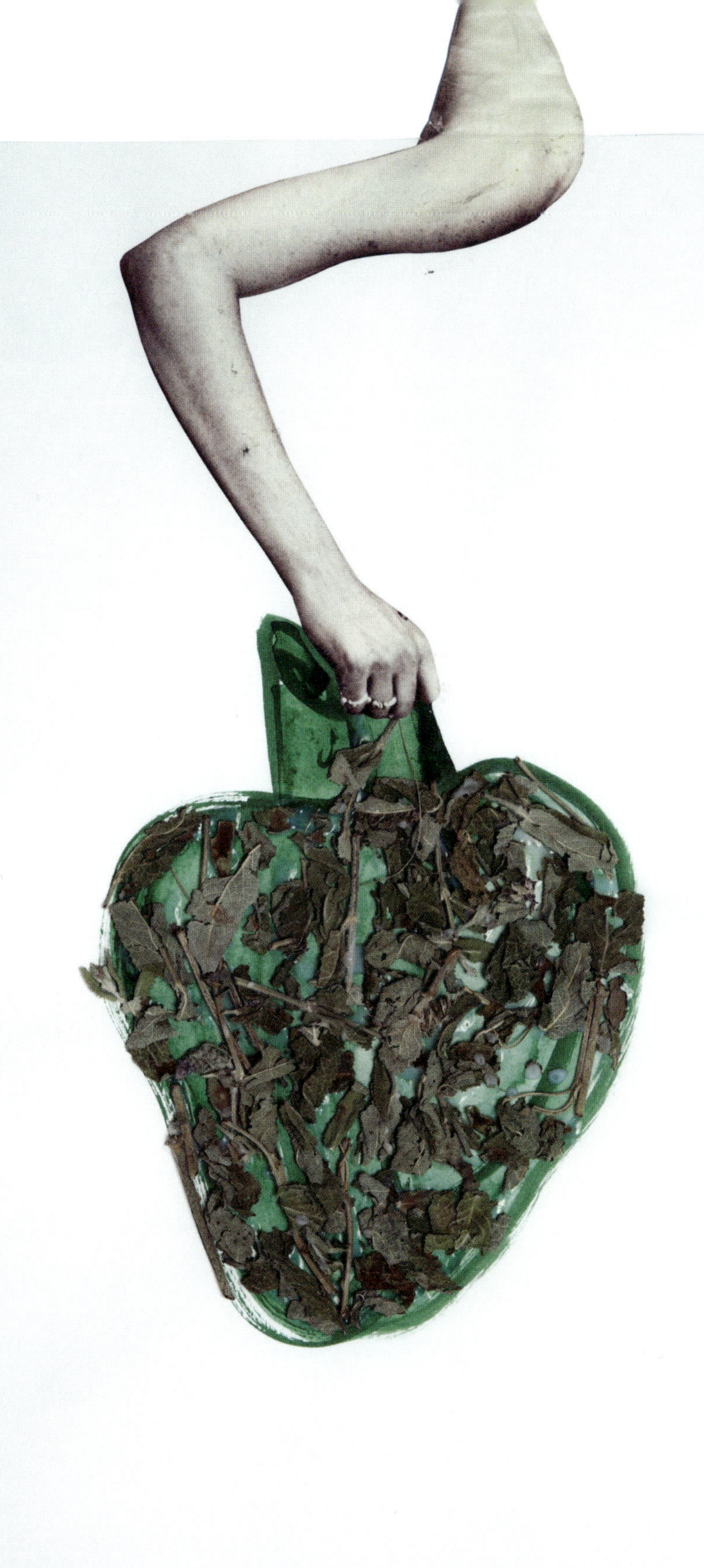

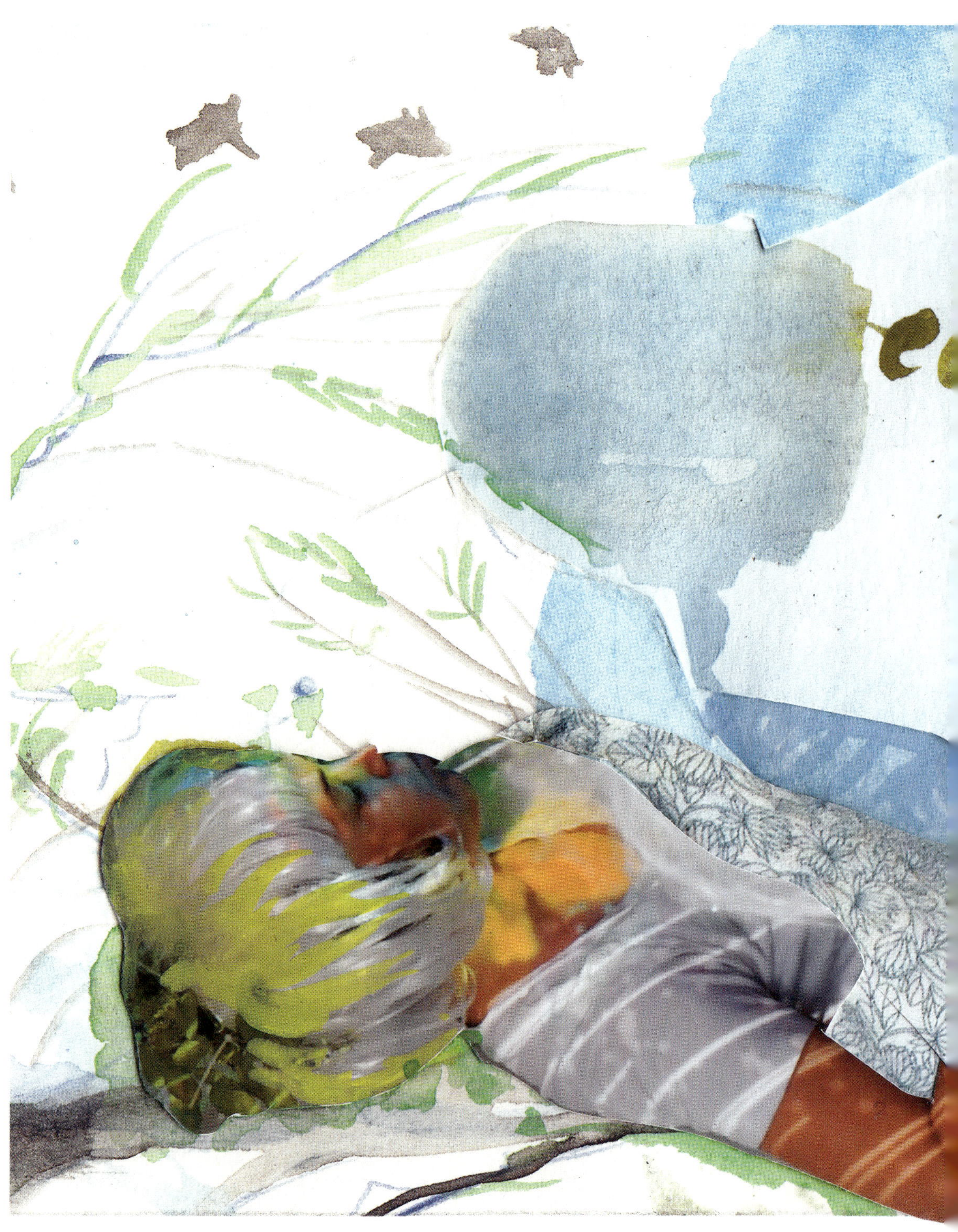

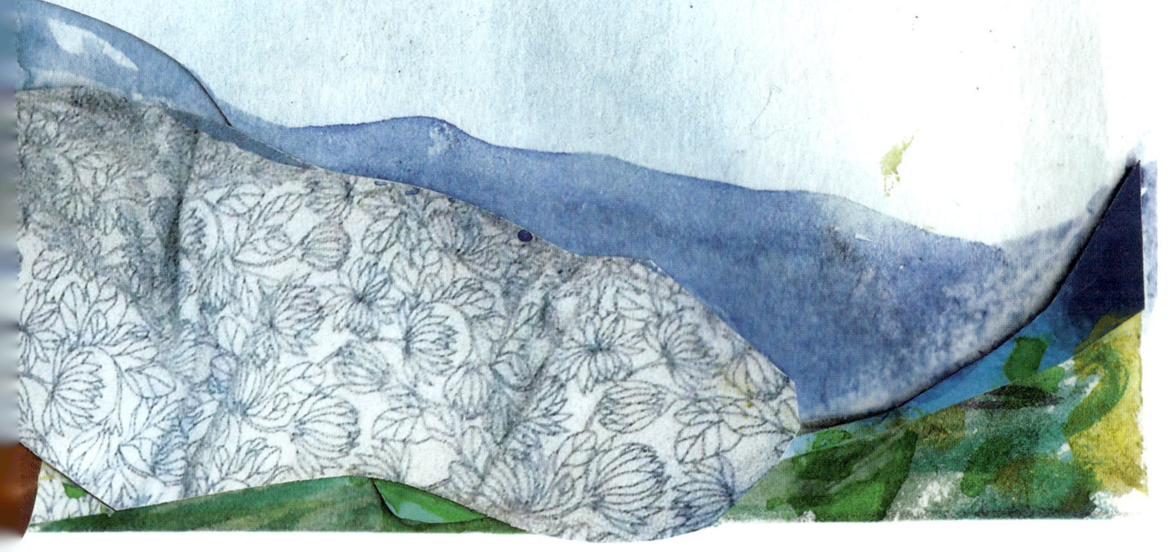
ting thistles

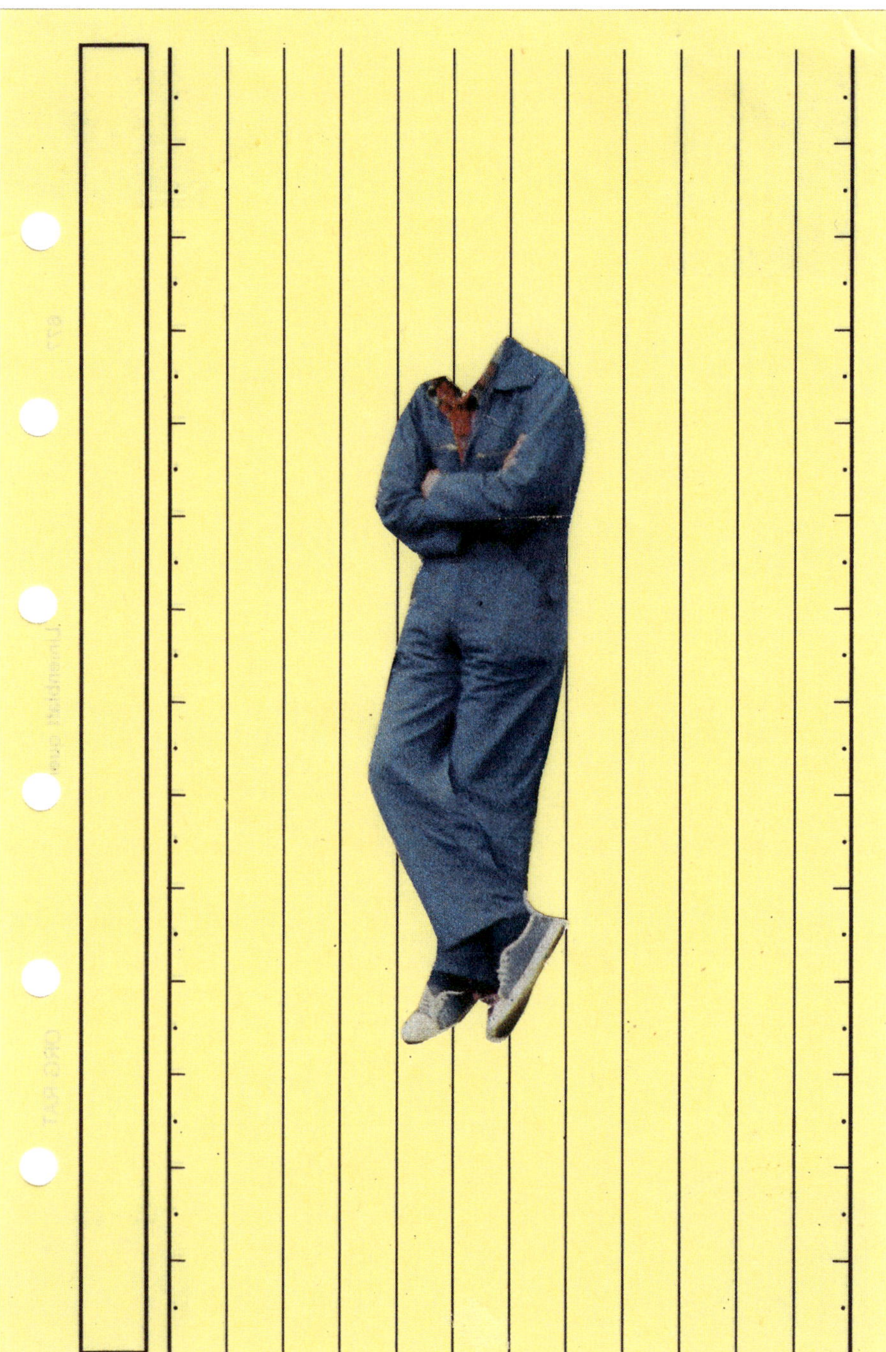

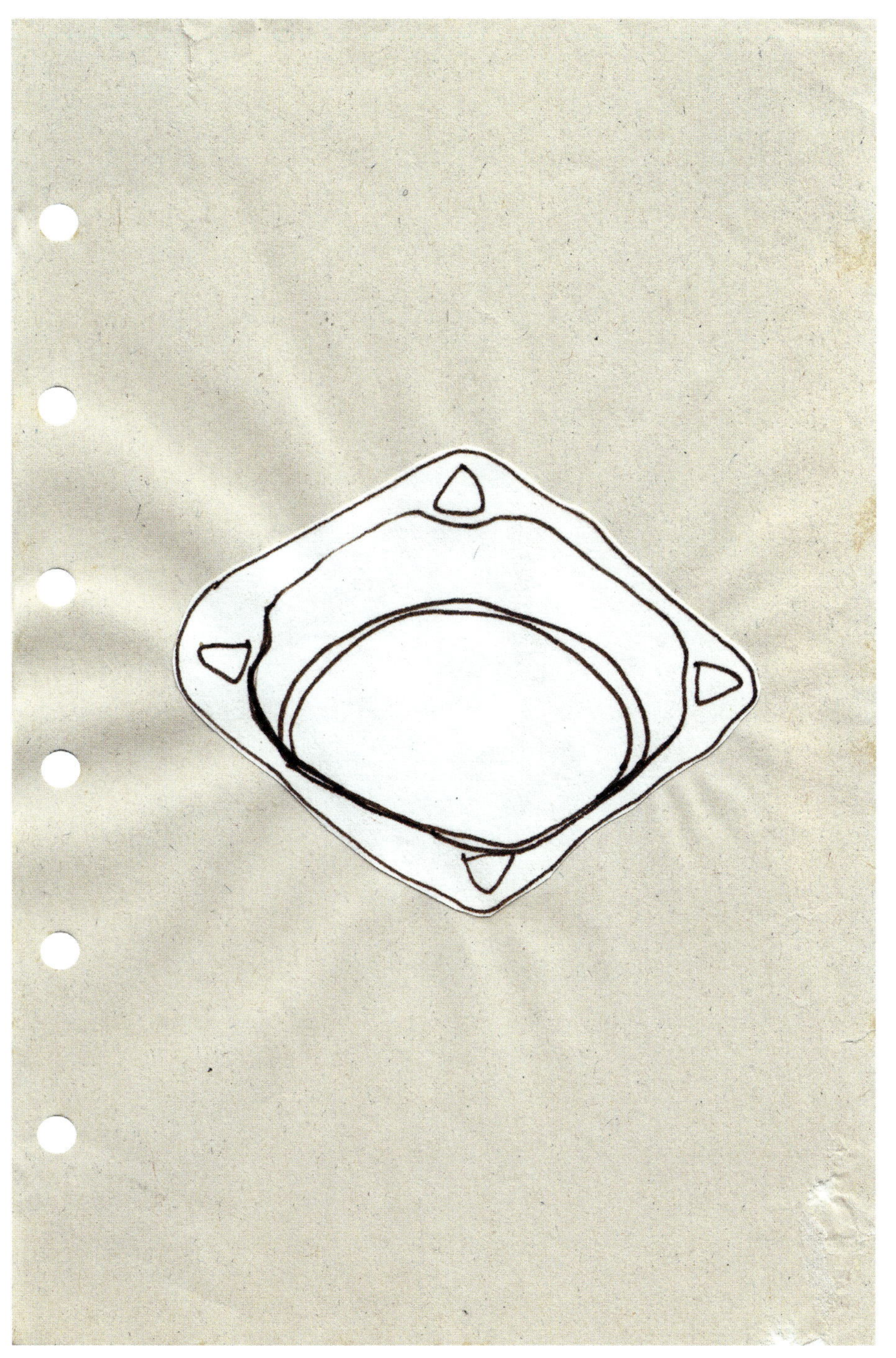

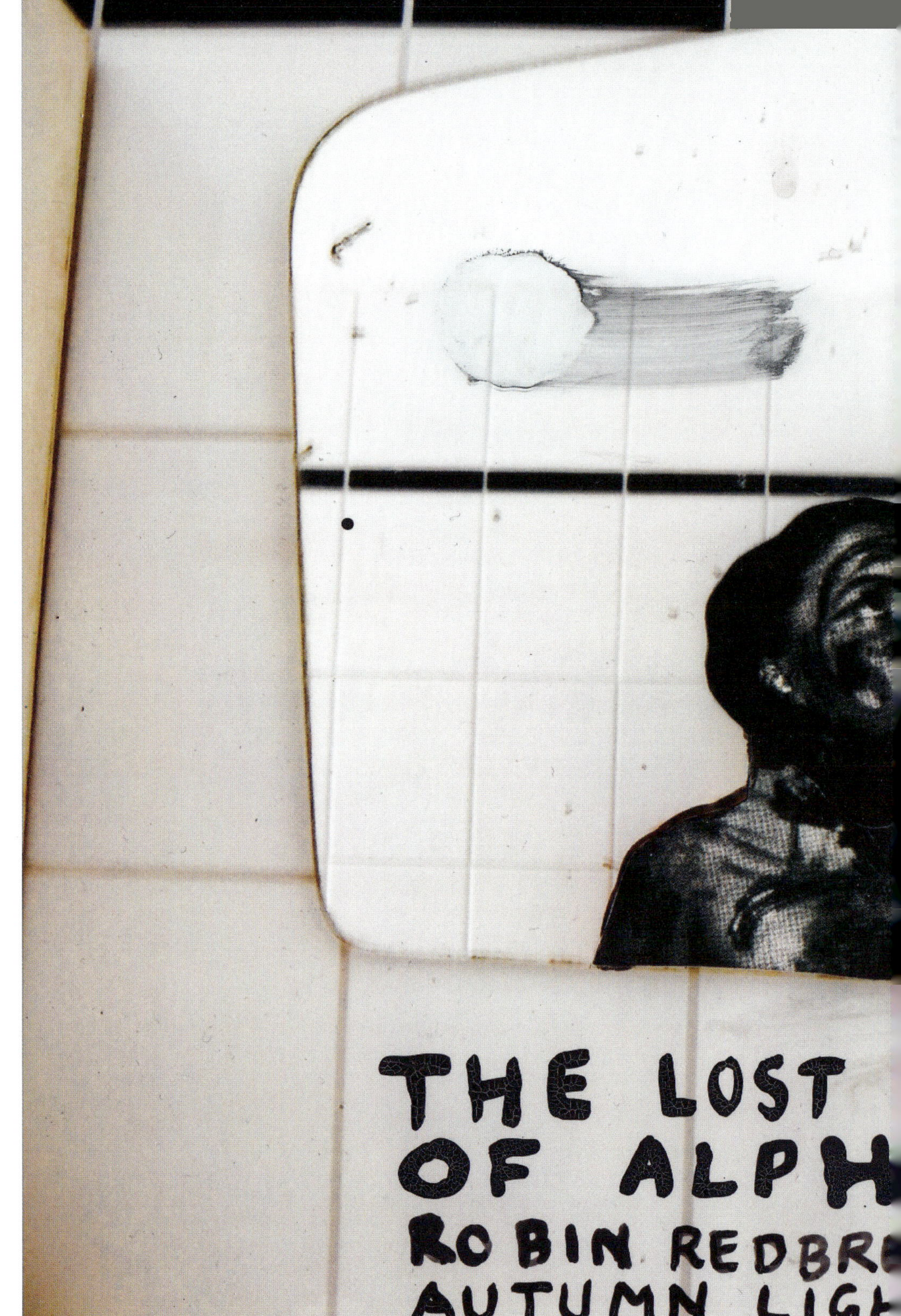
THE LOST
OF ALPH
ROBIN REDBRE
AUTUMN LIGH

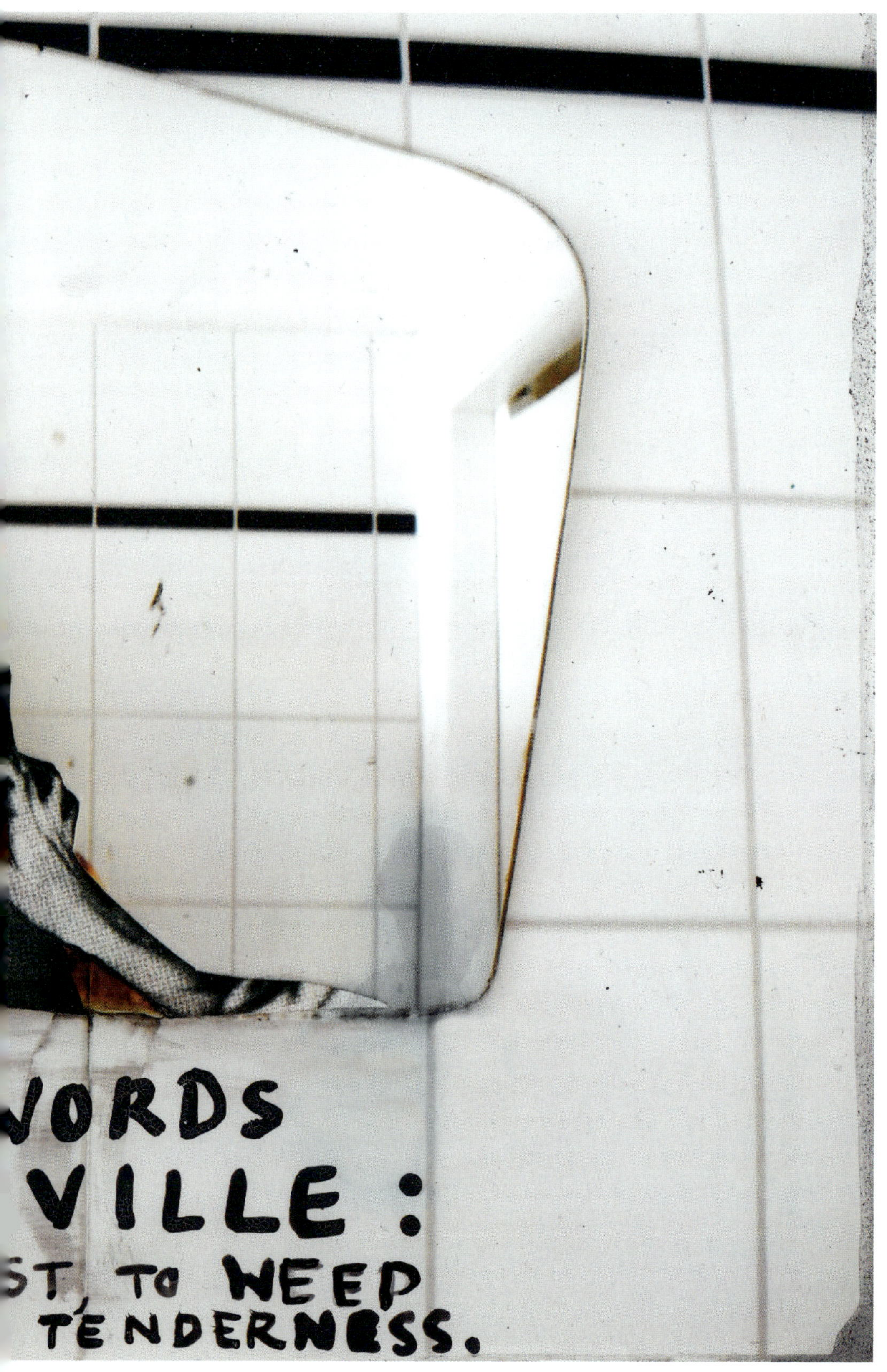

VORDS
VILLE :
ST TO WEEP
TENDERNESS.

BRUCE SPRINGSTEEN'S
PHRASE:

TRAMPS LIKE
US, BABY,
WE WERE
BORN TO
RUN...

(such a cliché, but I
can't help it)

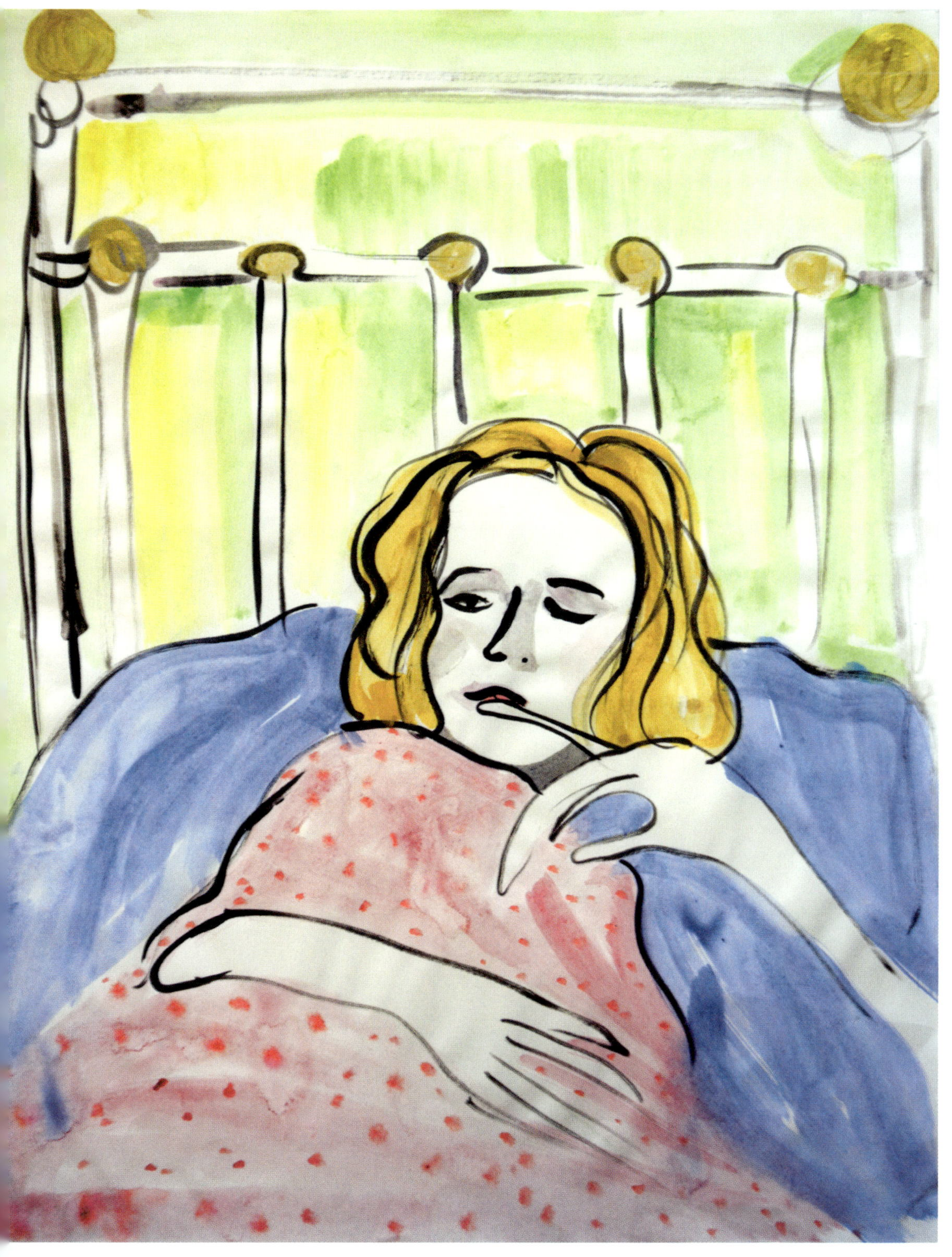

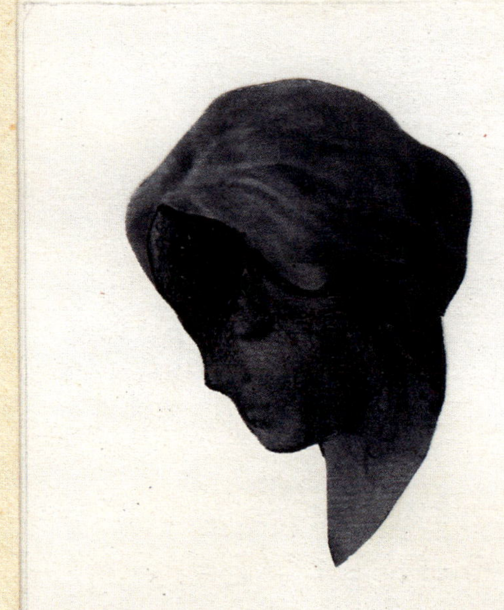

-the gorgeous Hammond-
sounding organ solo
in the Ben Harper
song "By My Side"

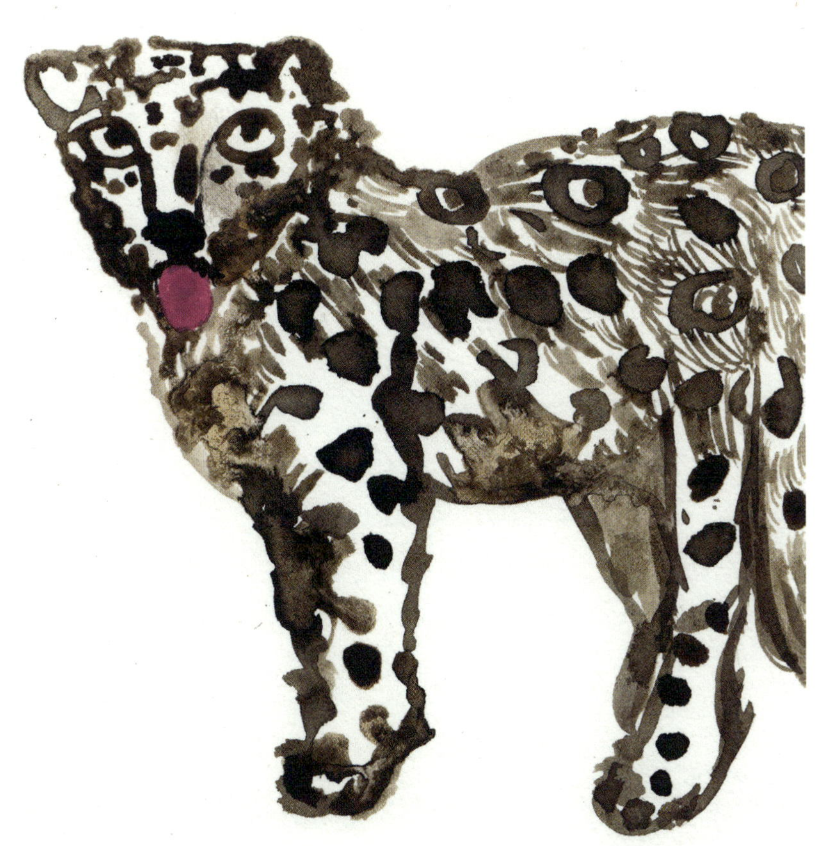

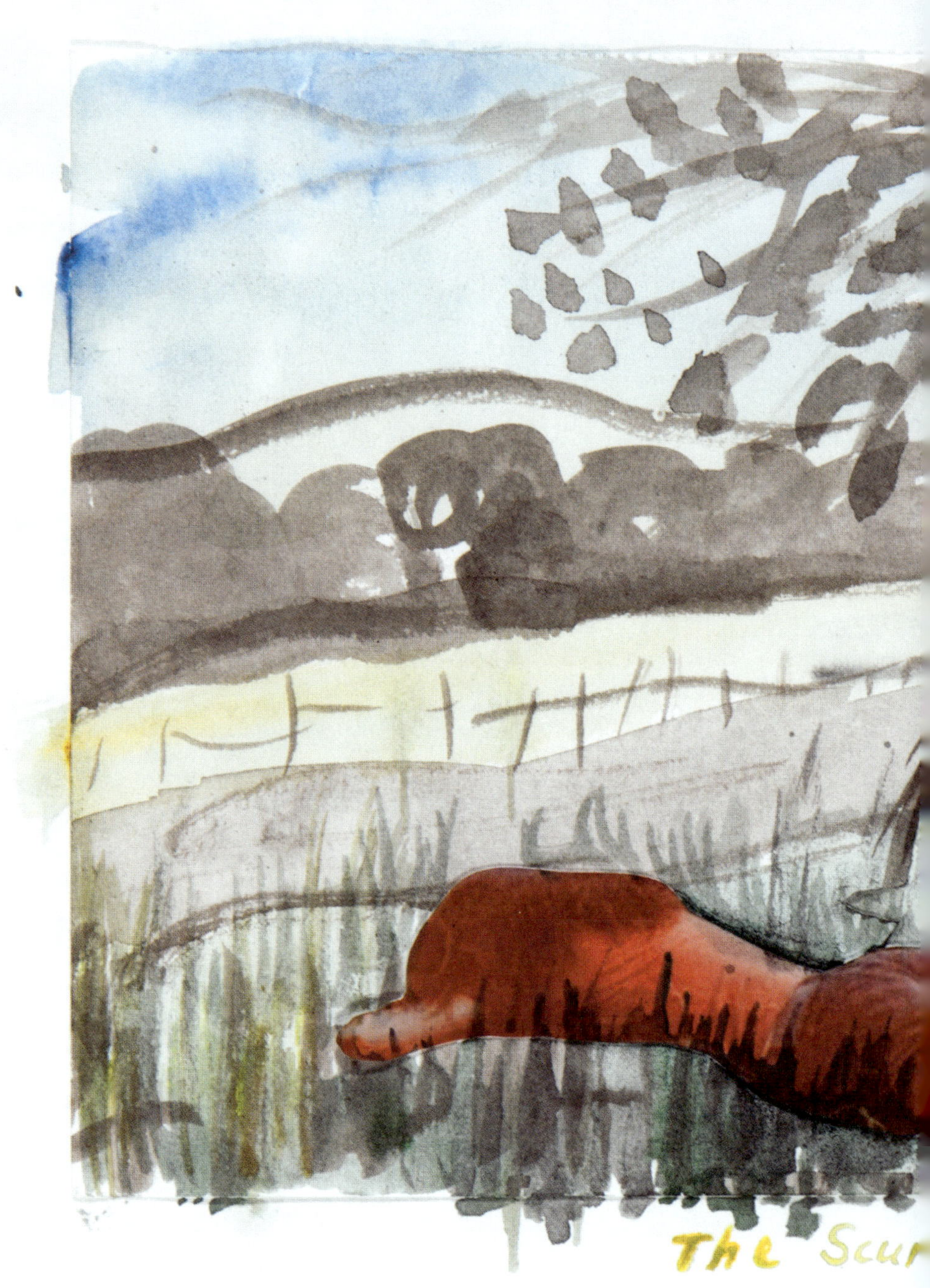

The Scur

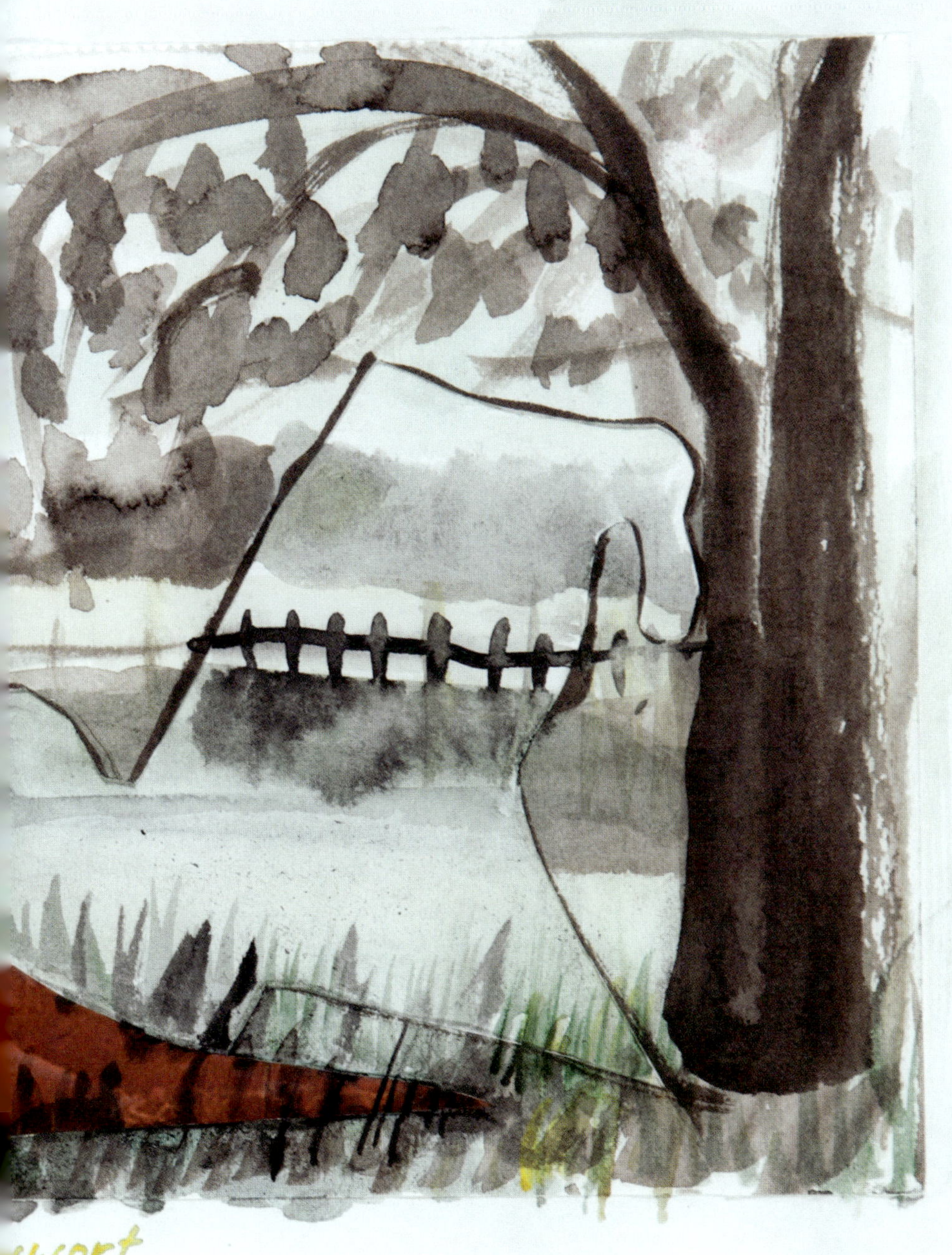

wort

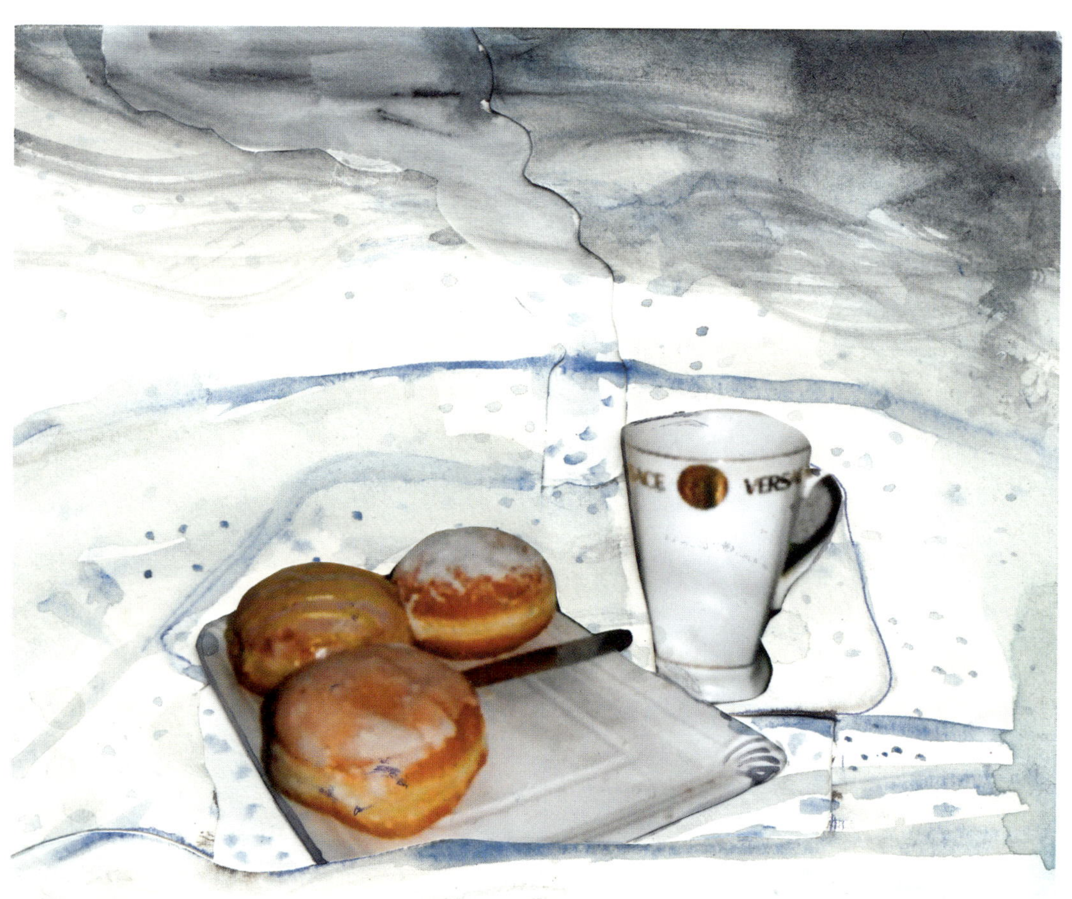

Letting the snowflakes cool down my coffee.

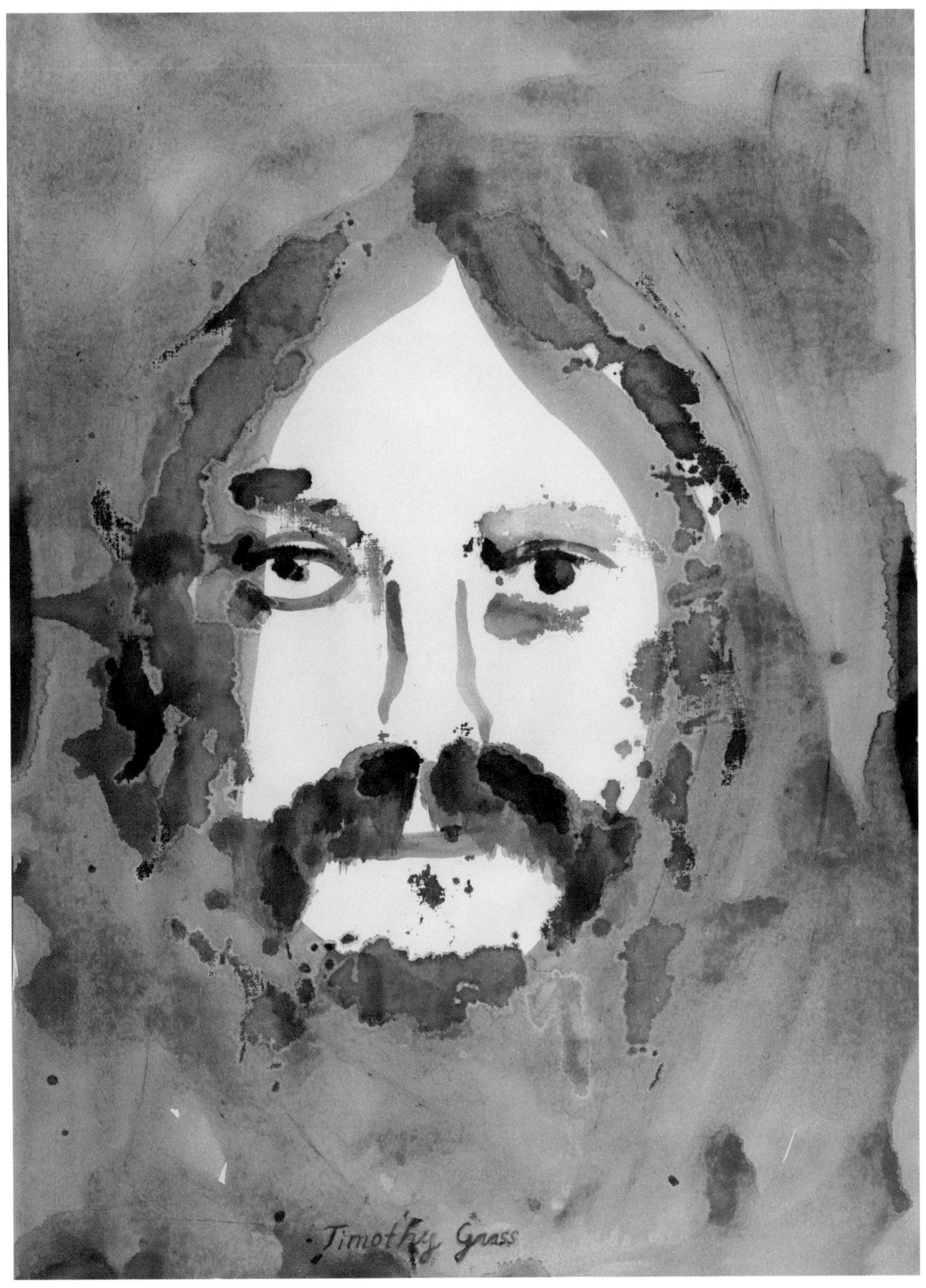

Timothy Grass

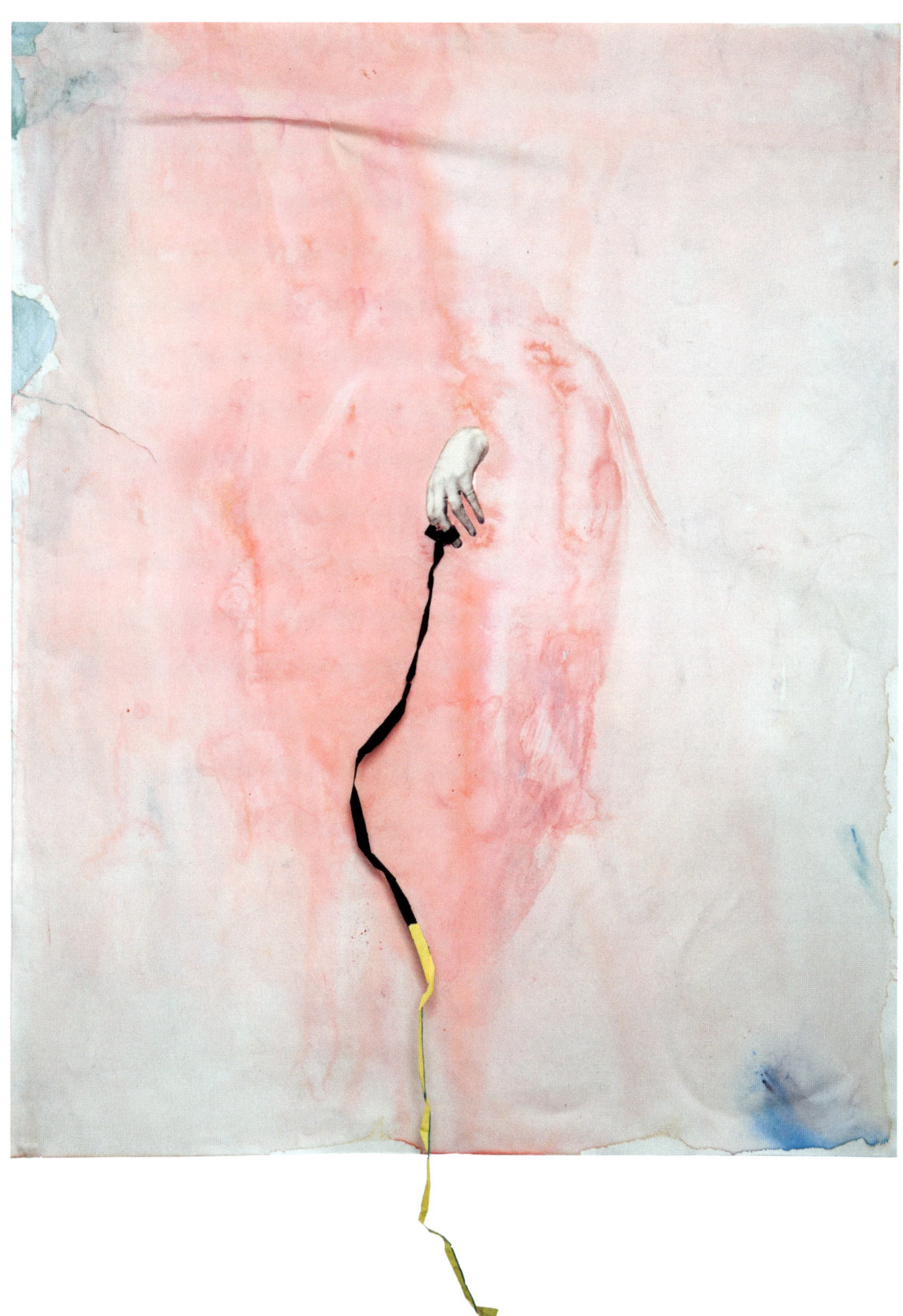

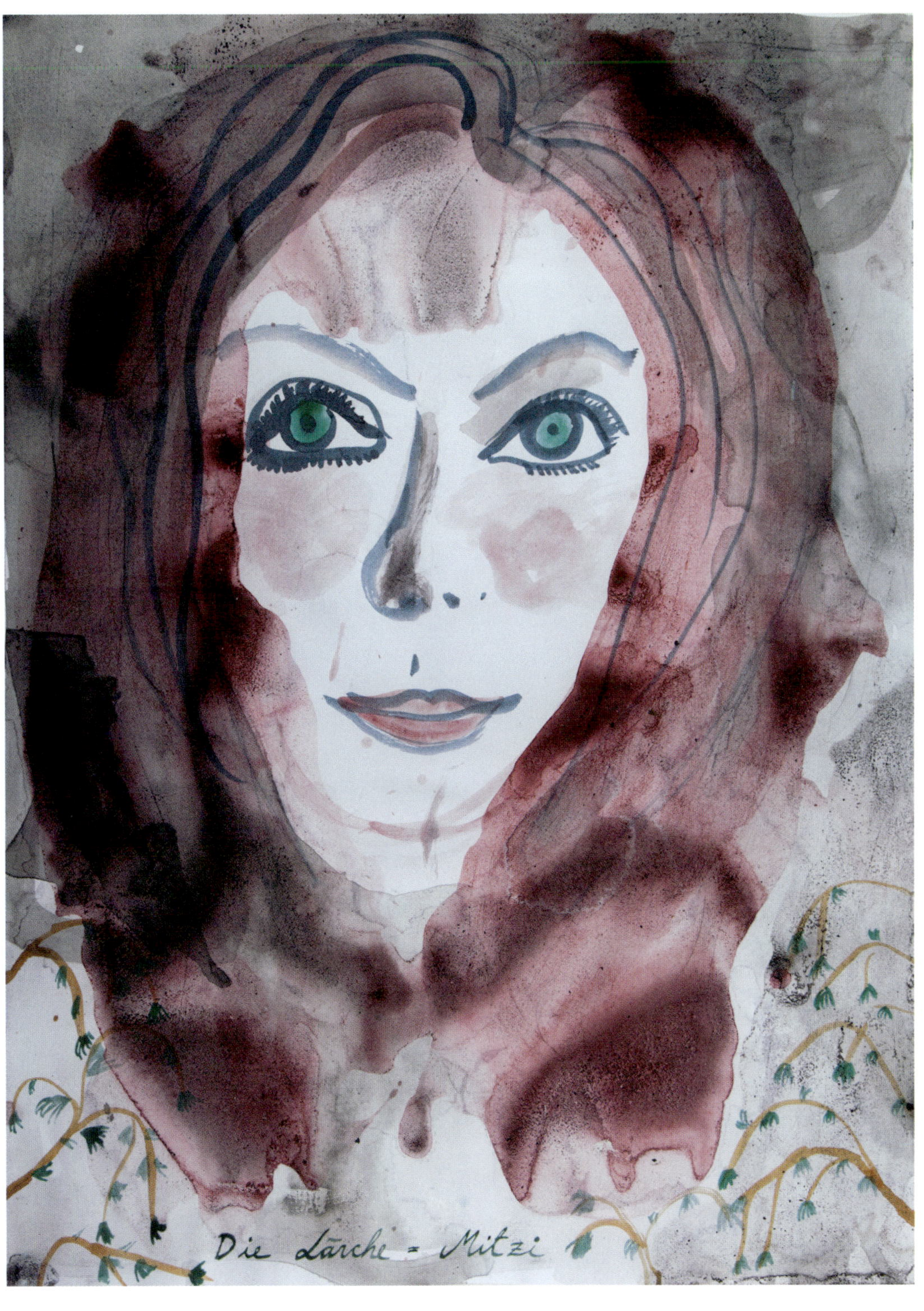

Die Lärche = Mitzi

I CAN NOT
COOK ANYMORE
AND USUALLY

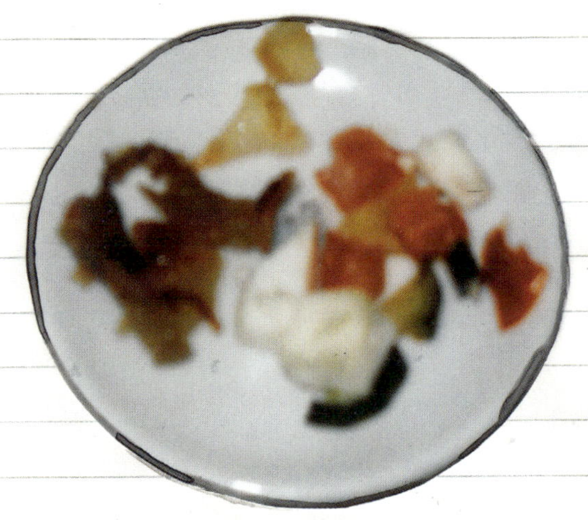

EATING MAKES
ME FEEL SAD

HEADACHE

CAUSING

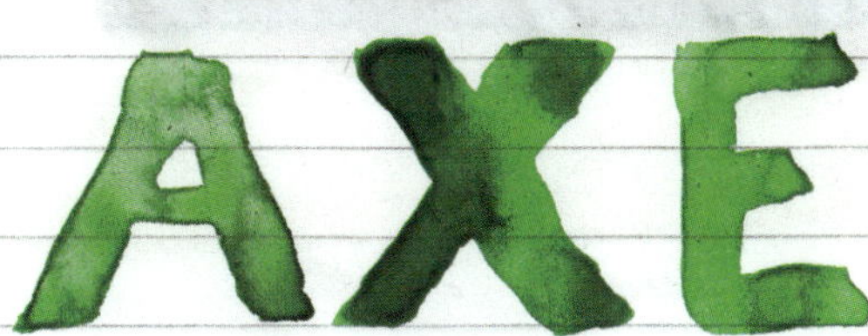

AXE

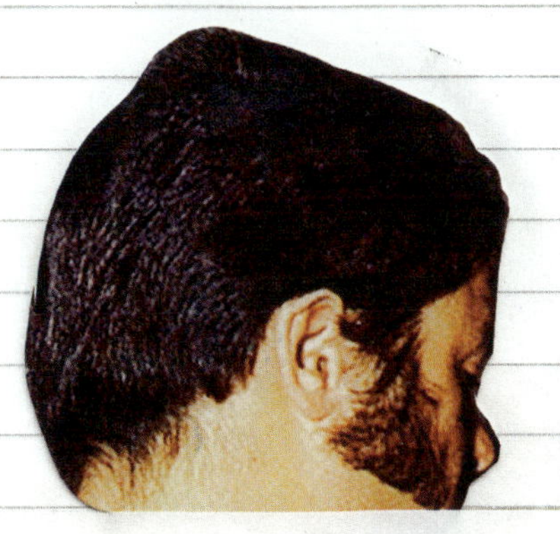

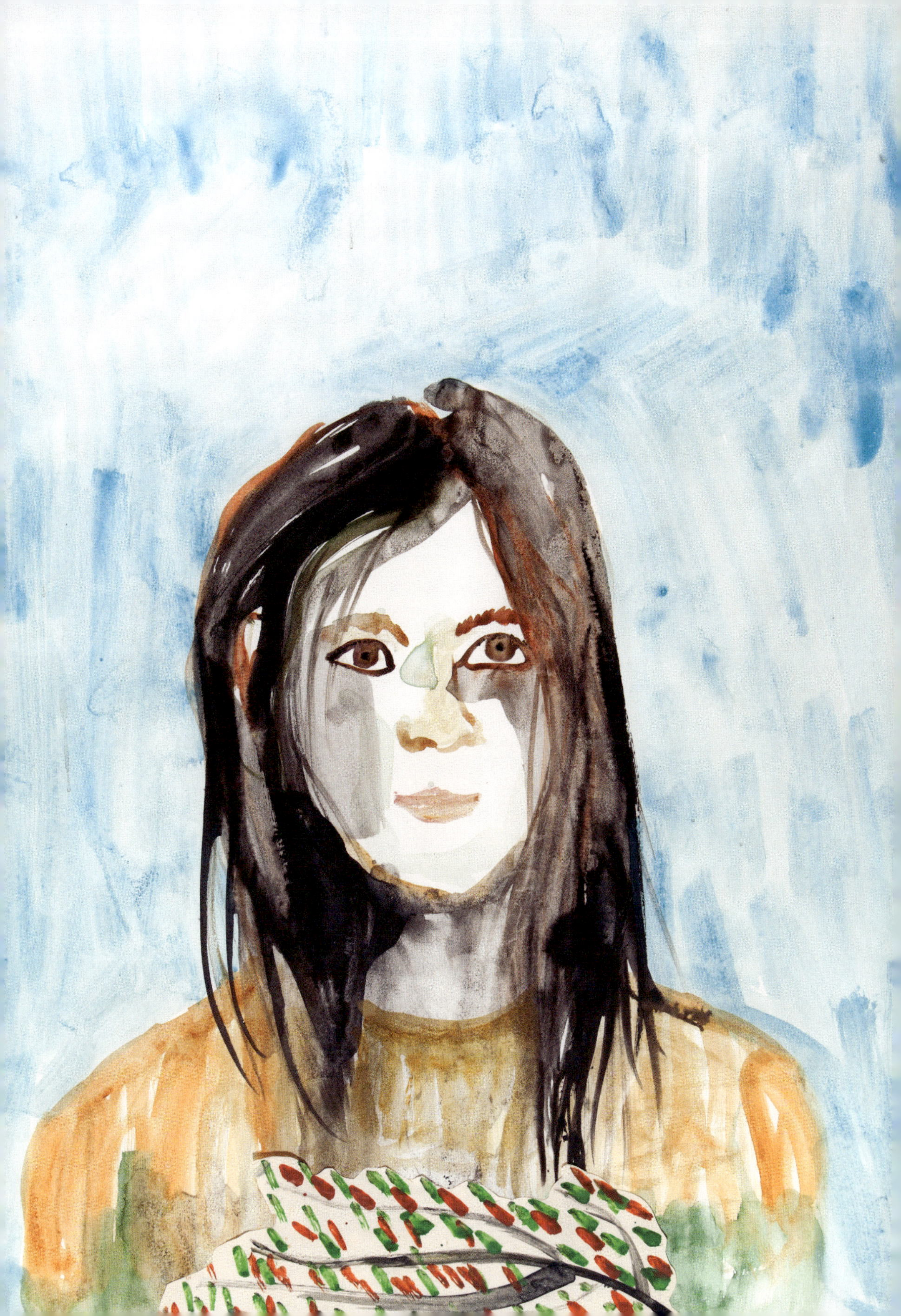

- PUTTING ON PERFUME
- EATING RAW FISH
- TESTING NEW PERFUMES
- PASSING BY SÖRNÄINEN

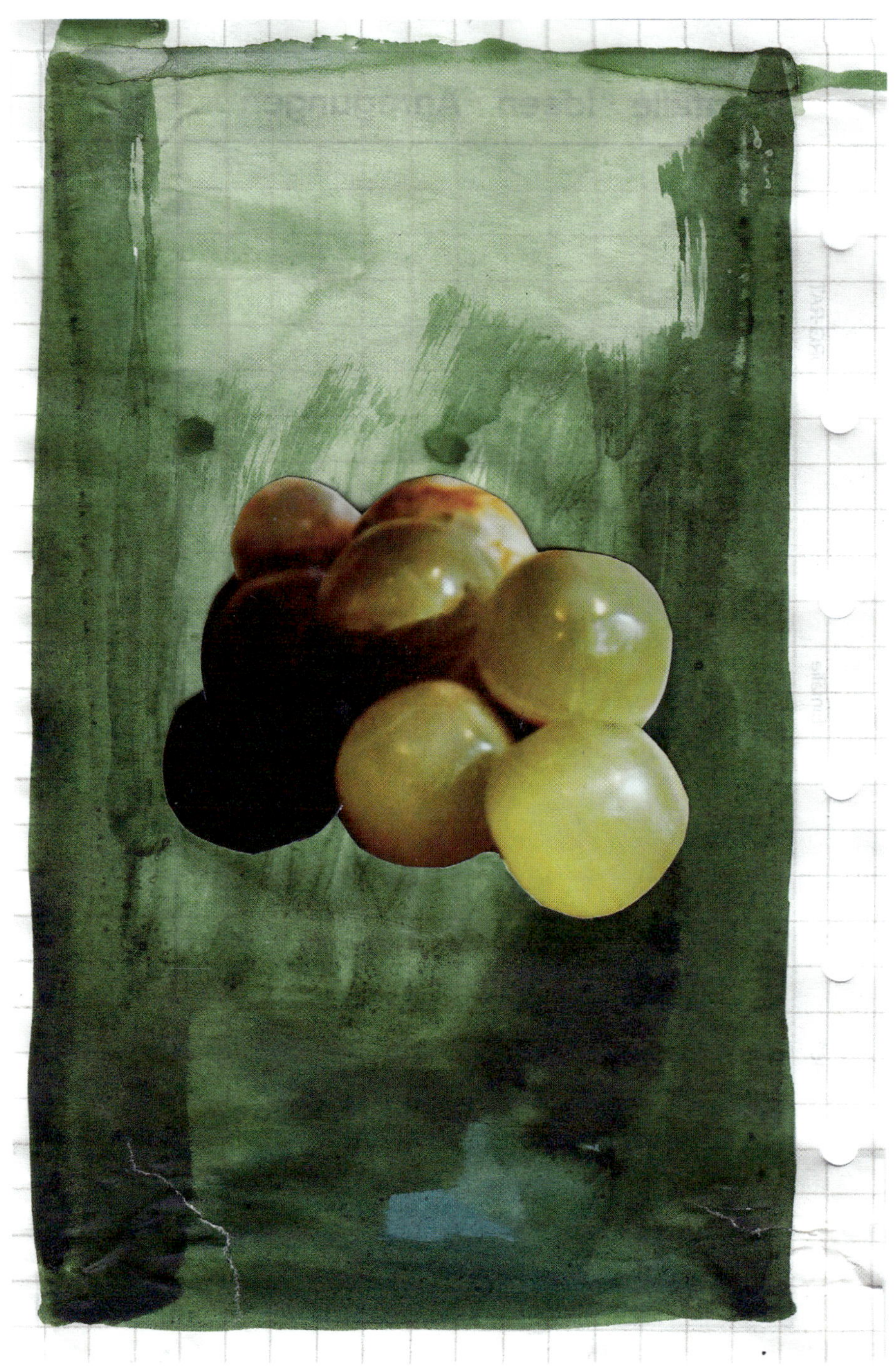

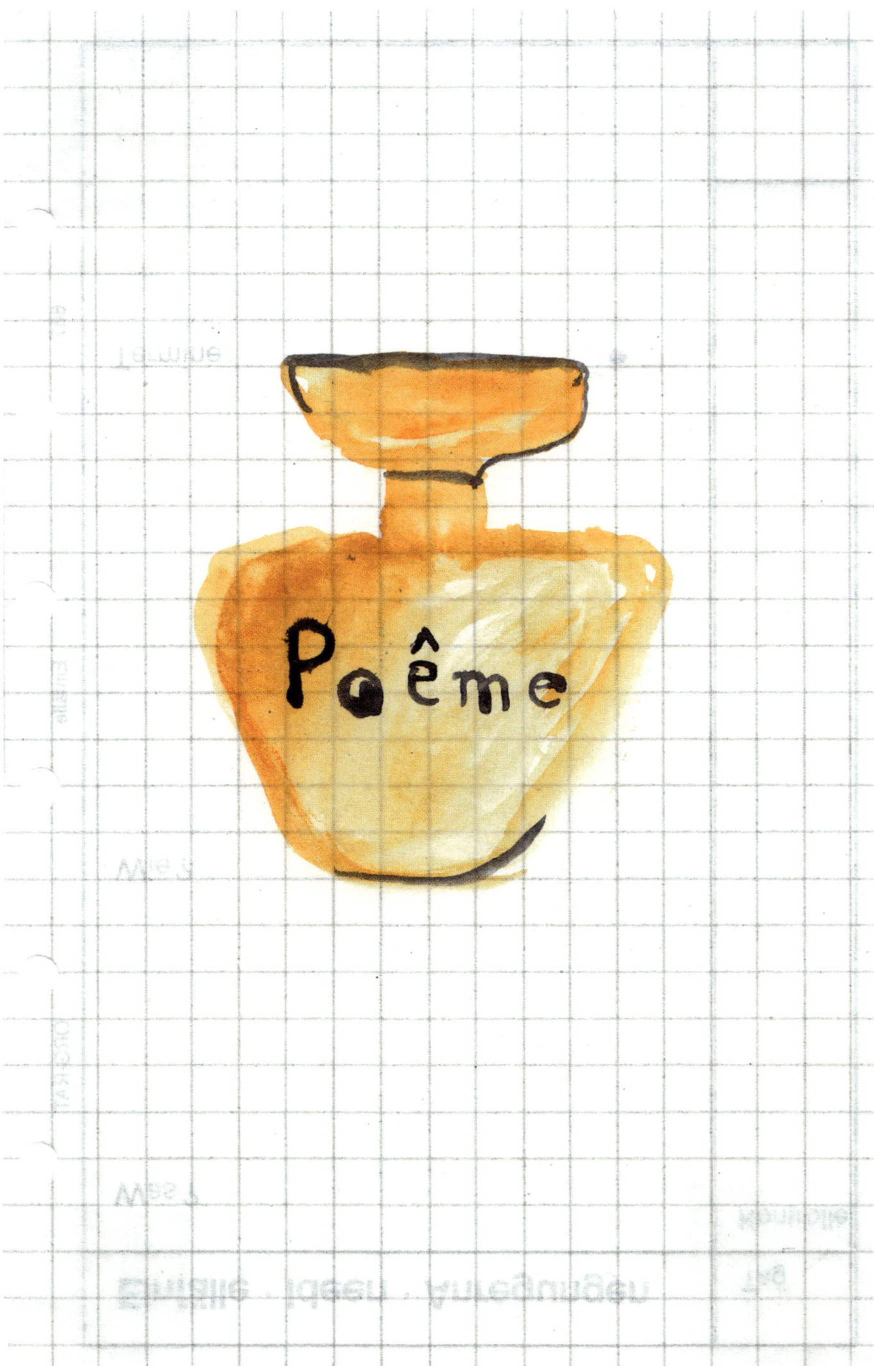
Poême

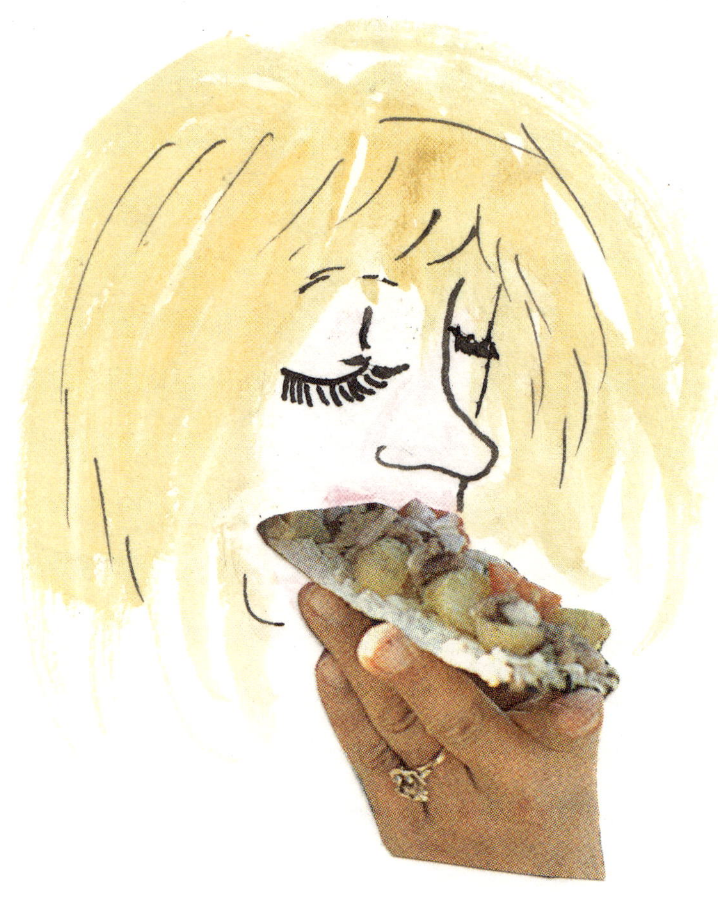

egg – anchovy – sandwich

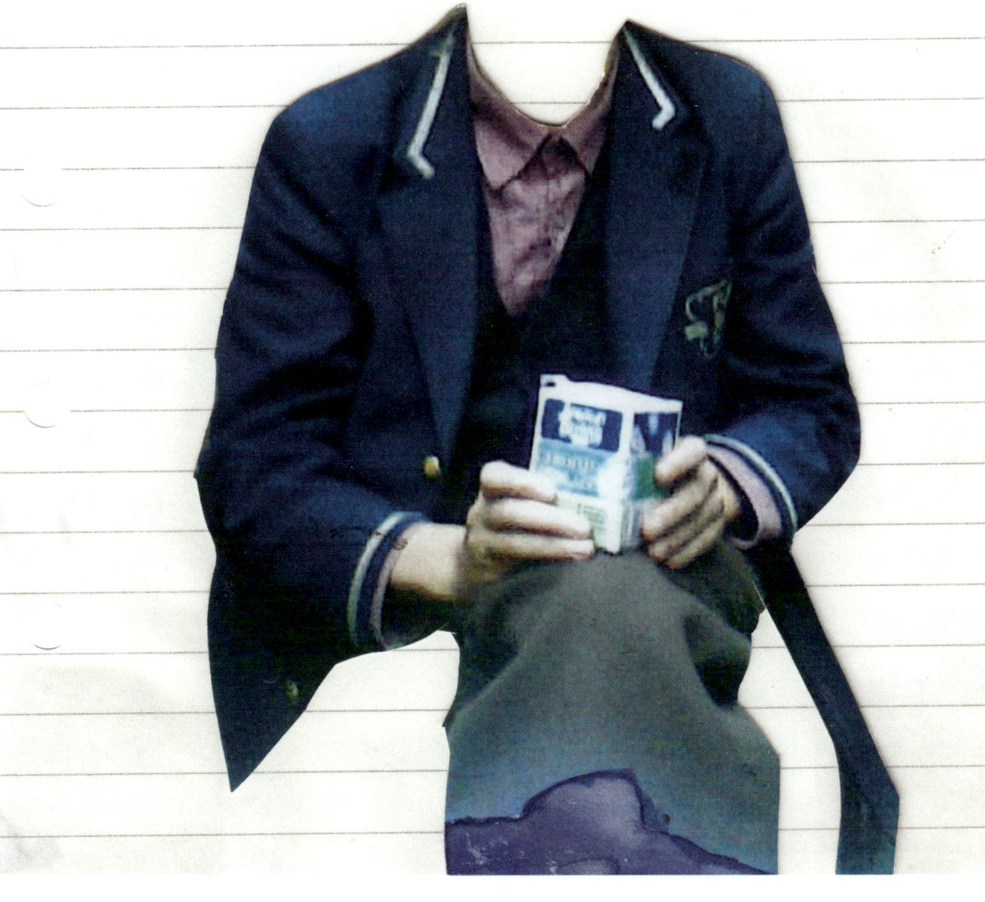
EVERY MOTORBIKE,
IT'S HIS.

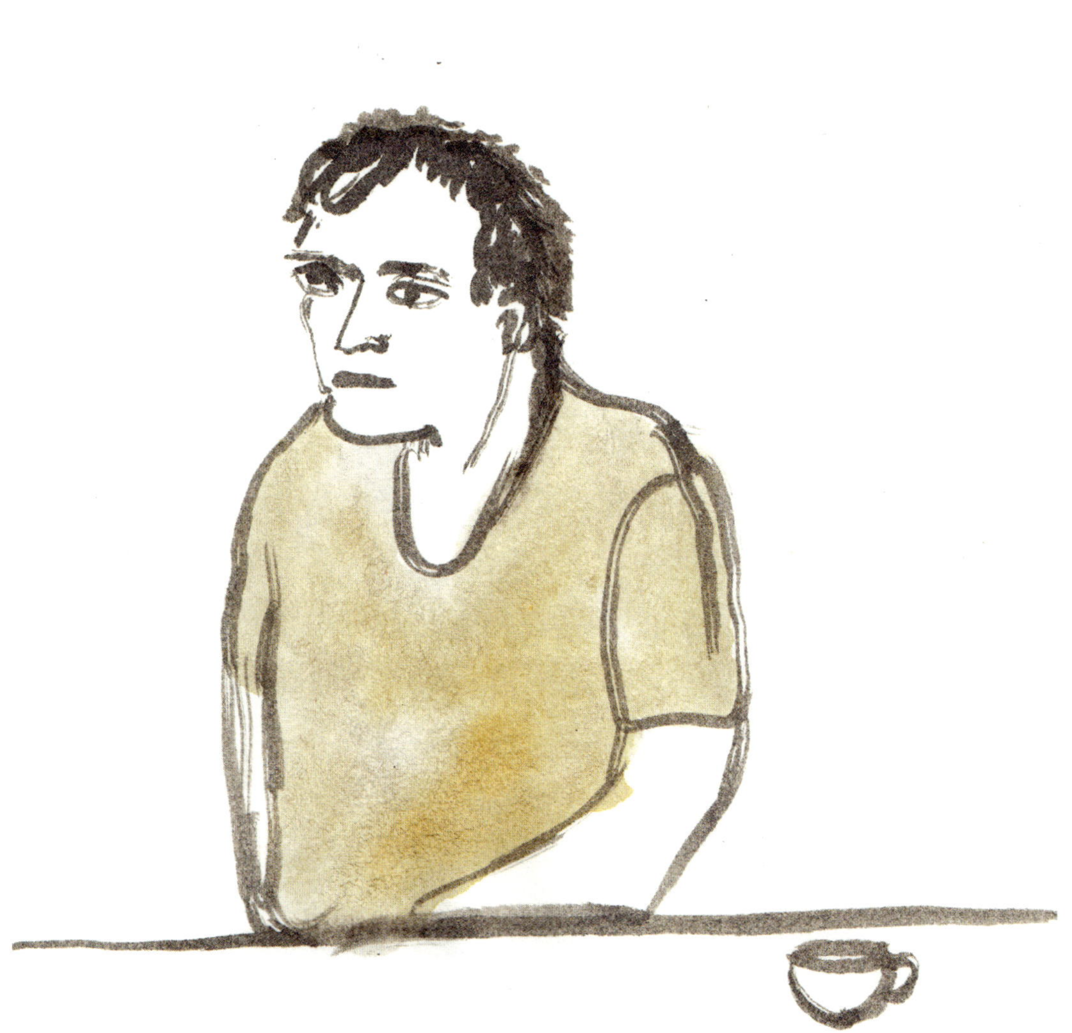

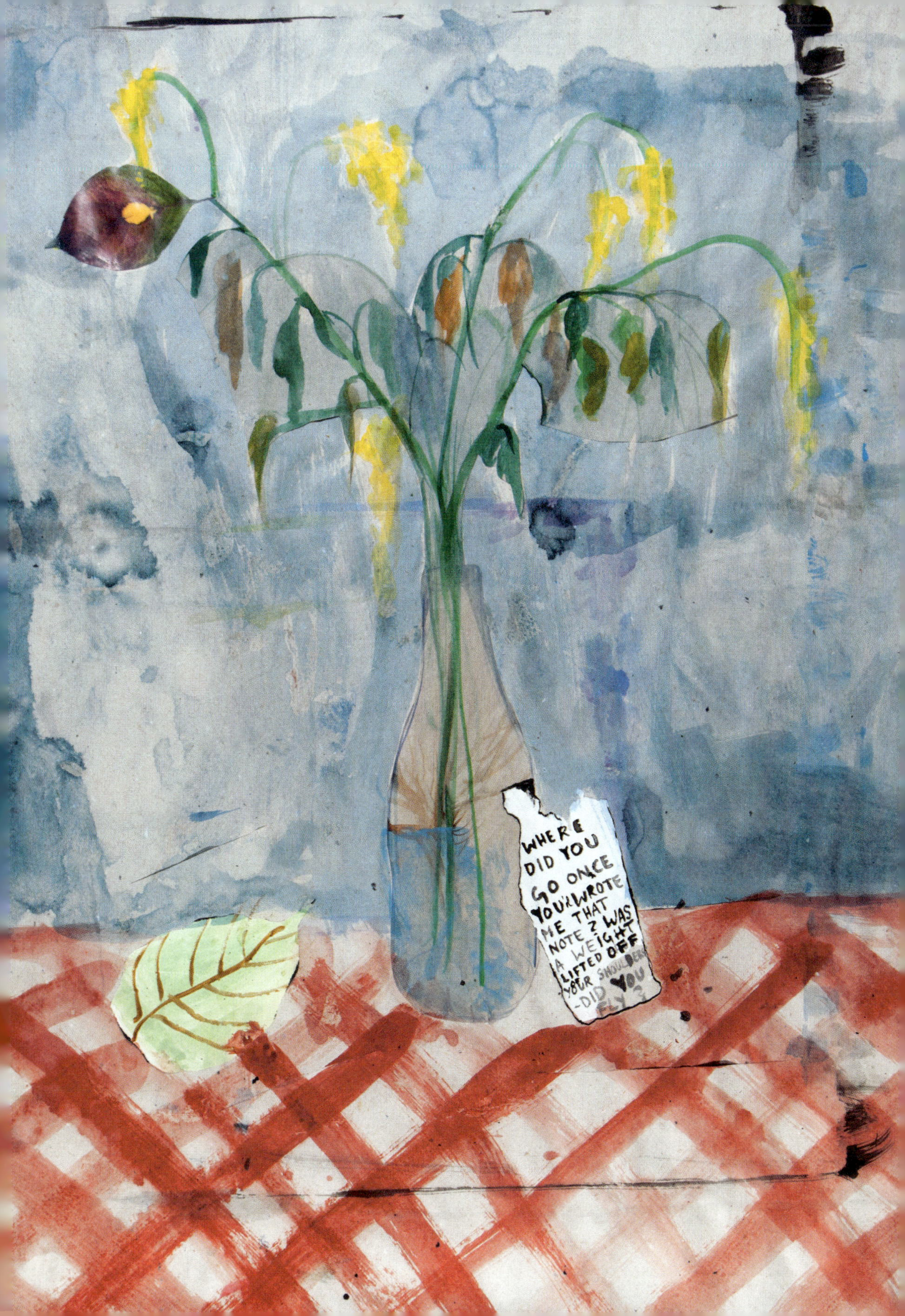

WHERE
DID YOU
GO ONCE
YOU'R WROTE
ME THAT
NOTE Z WAS
A WEIGHT
LIFTED OFF
YOUR SHOULDERS
-DID YOU
FLY ?

The Anjala c

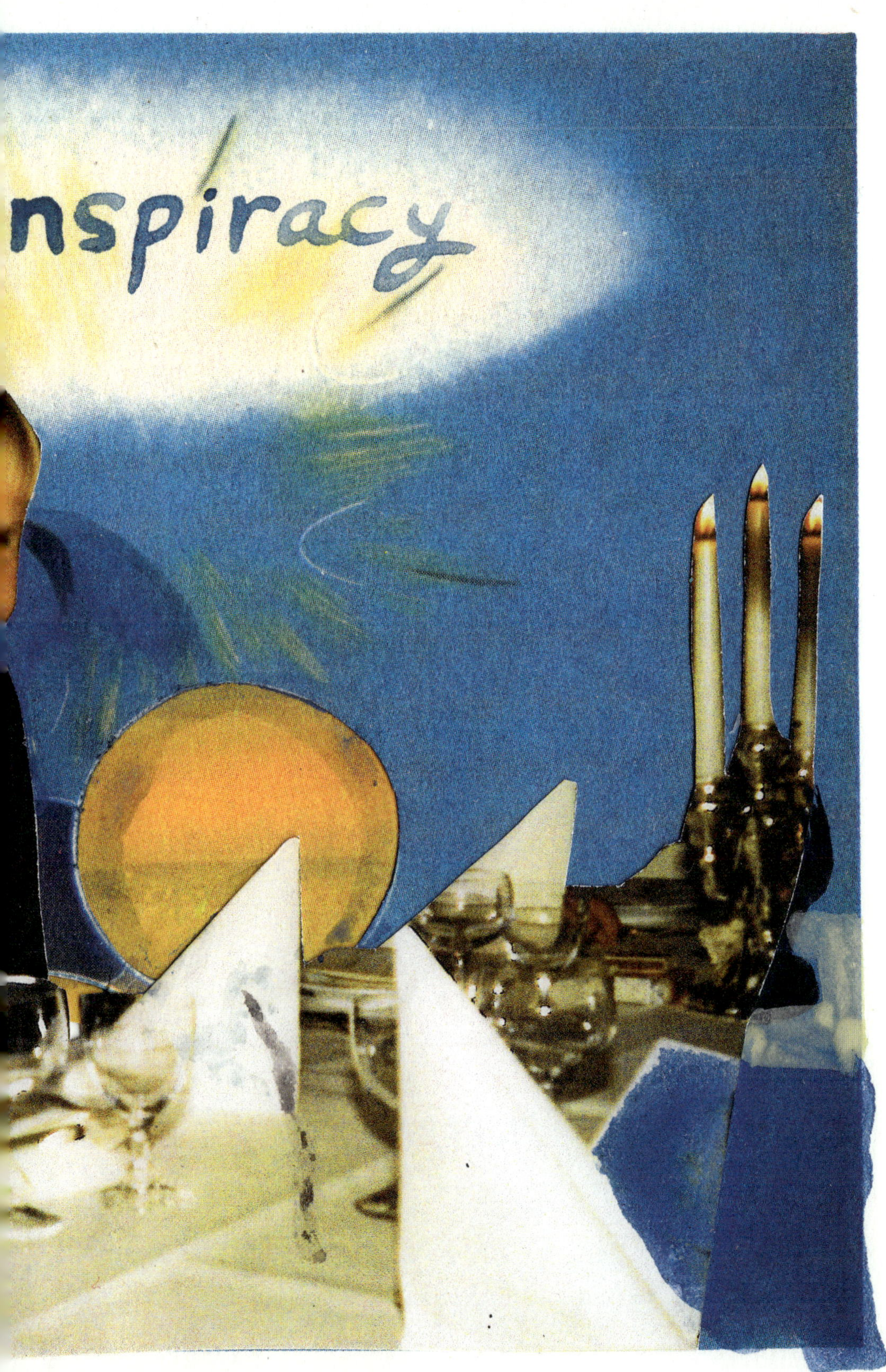
nspiracy

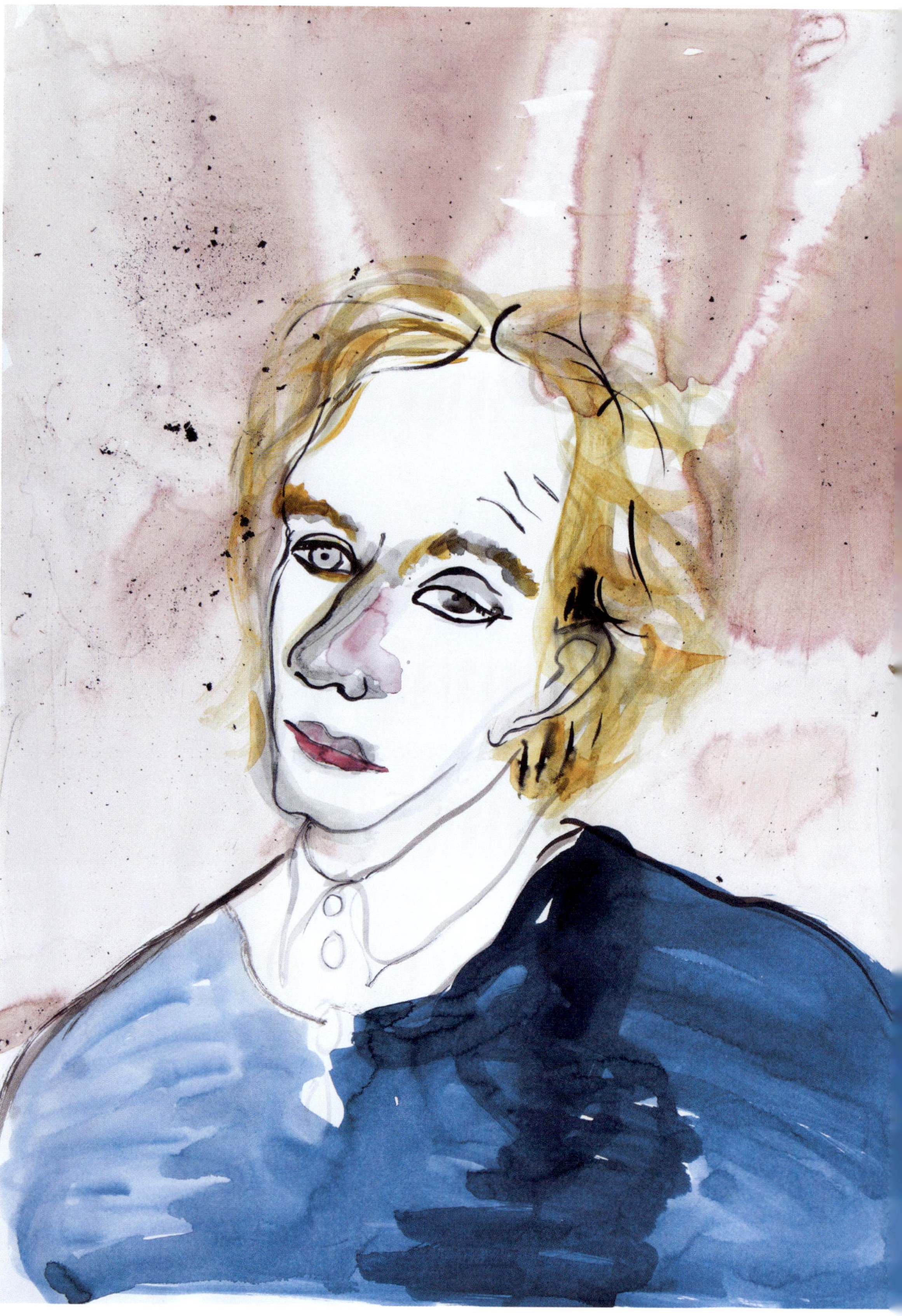

THE HELSINKI BALTIC HERRING FAIR

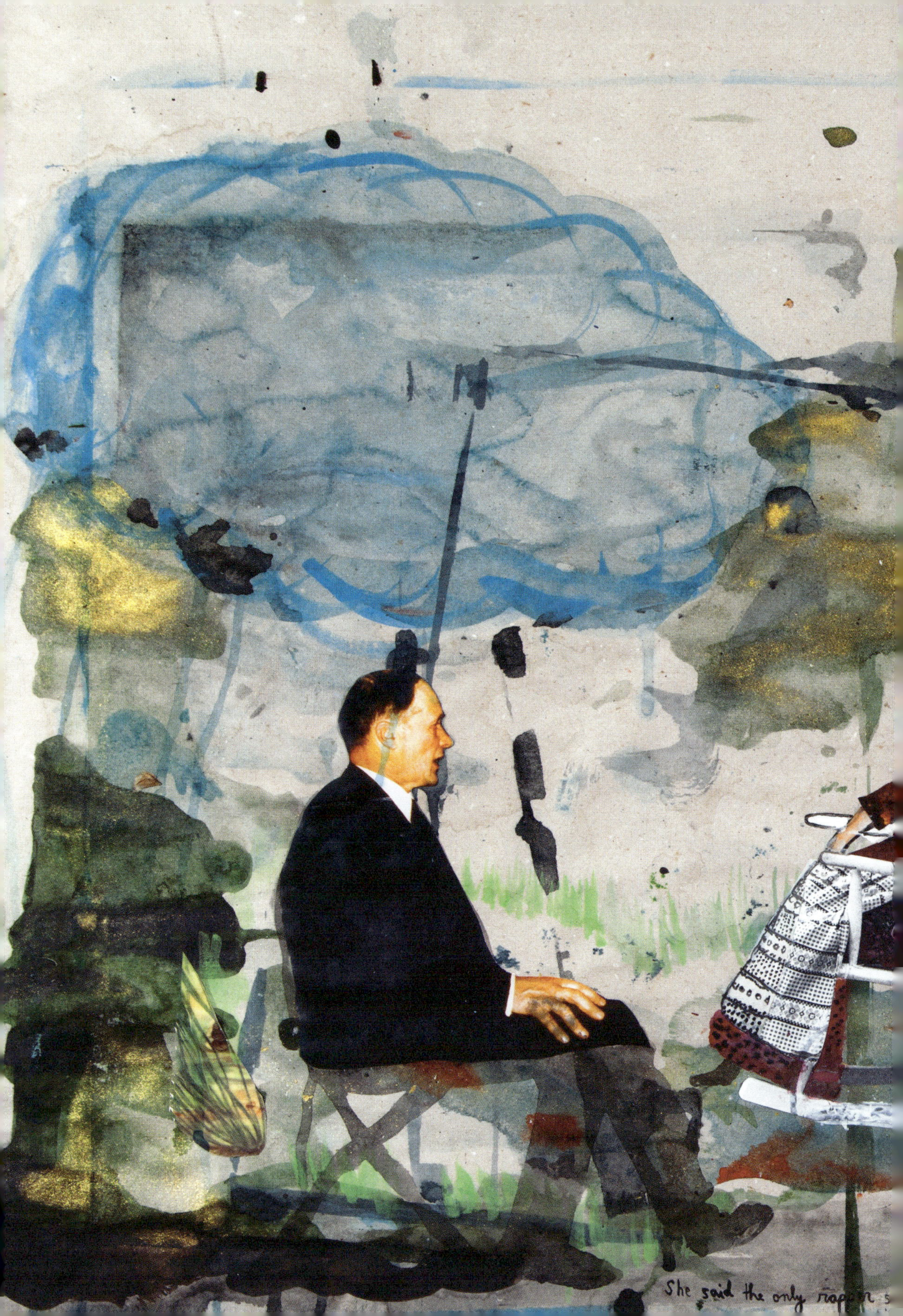
She said the only napkins

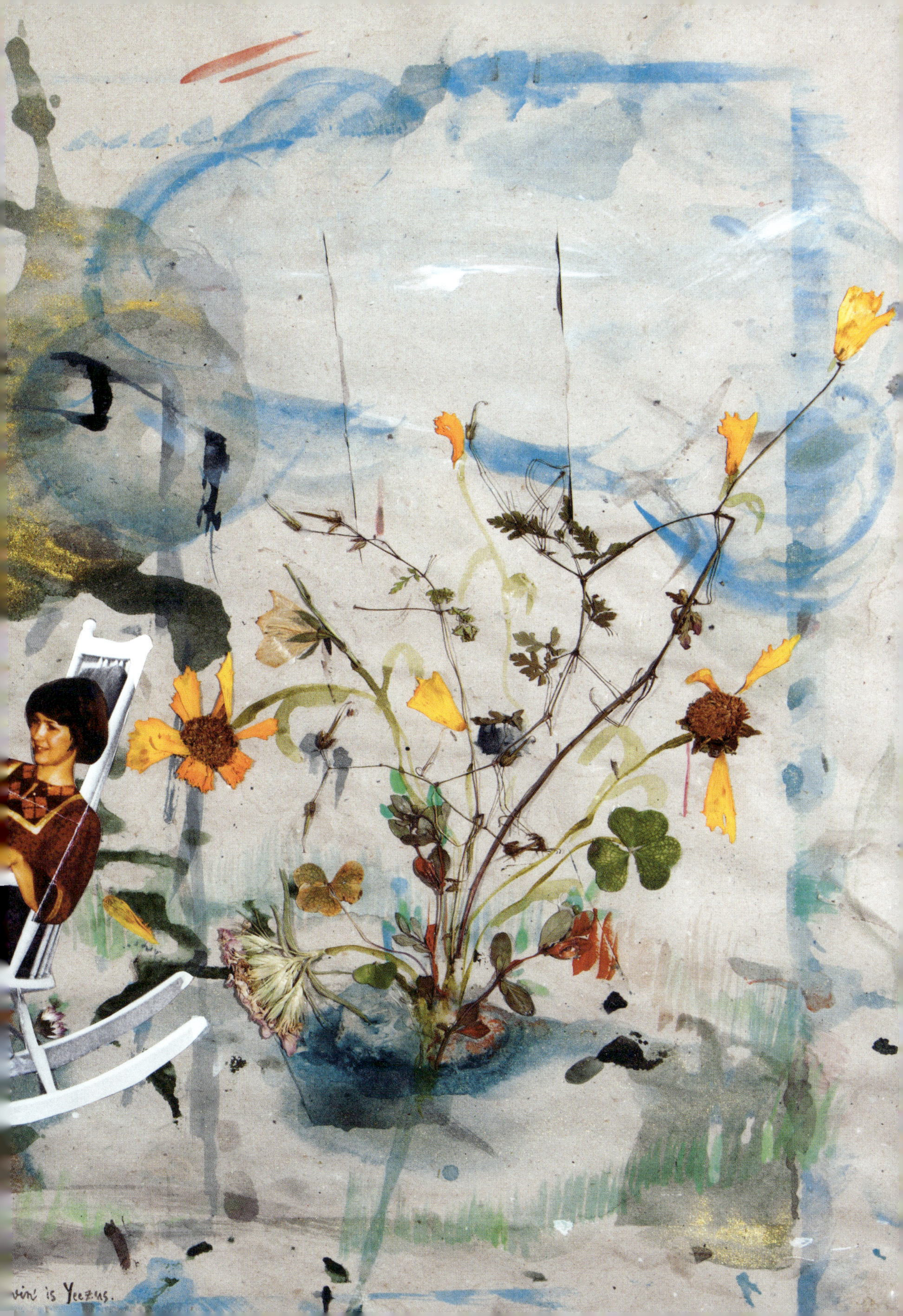
vin' is Yeezus.

Even though this "thing„ ended
last week I could still mention
a few things that remind
me of you... because you
are the **LAST ONE** I had a
connection **WITH AND** felt I
belonged to:

- **The BIG, HOME** in Ullanlinna
- That **CERTAIN BENCH** at
TÖÖLÖNLAHTI - BAY where
we **HAD OUR FIRST DATE**
- **YOU LOSING YOUR
NERVE FOR** NO REASON
if **YOU ARE TENSE**
- **IDIOTIC COMBINA-
TIONS OF CLOTHES
THAT I WAS ASHAMED OF
LIKE THE 90s SLING
BACKPACK AND** the
chequered trousers from the 70s

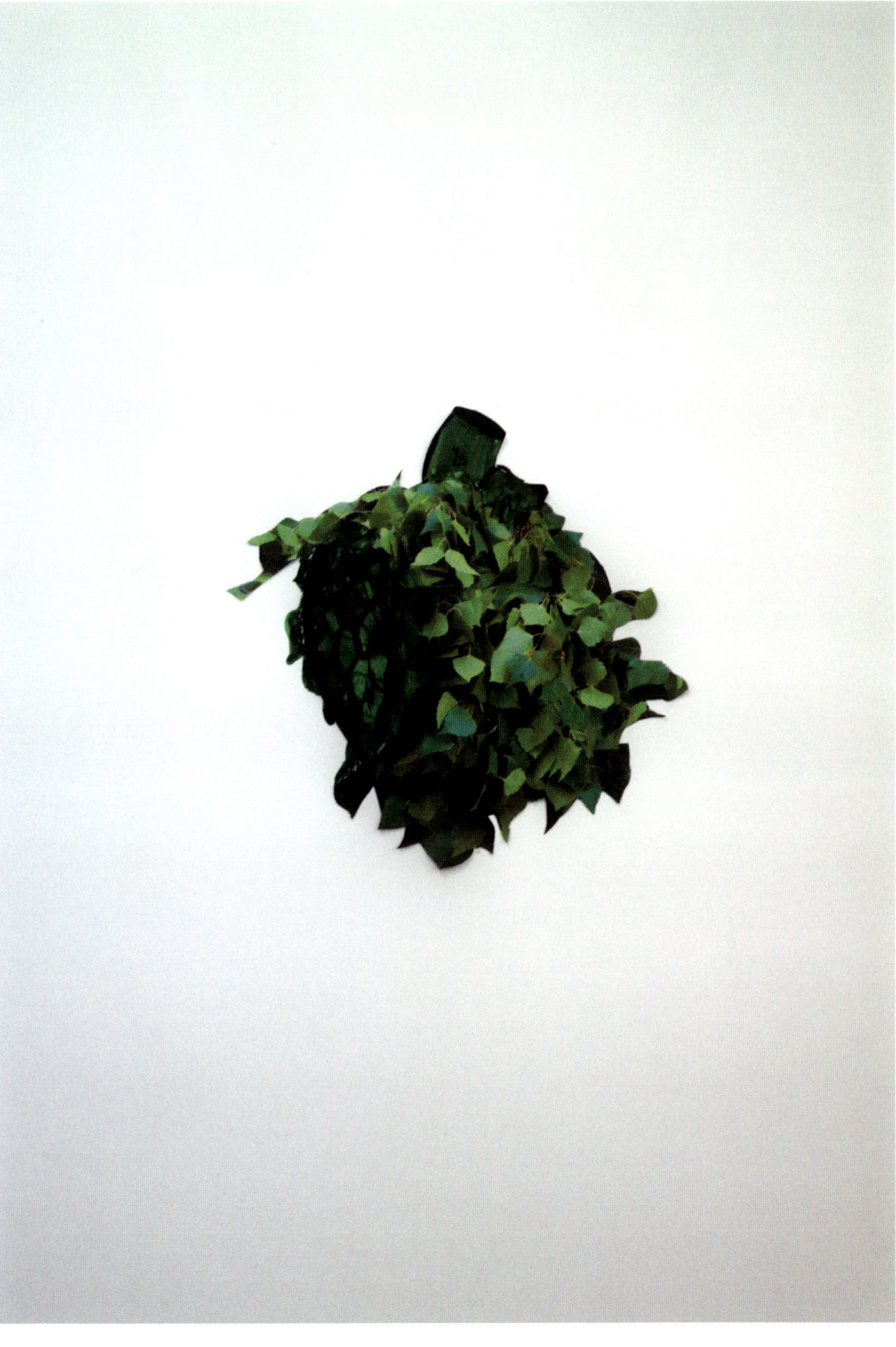

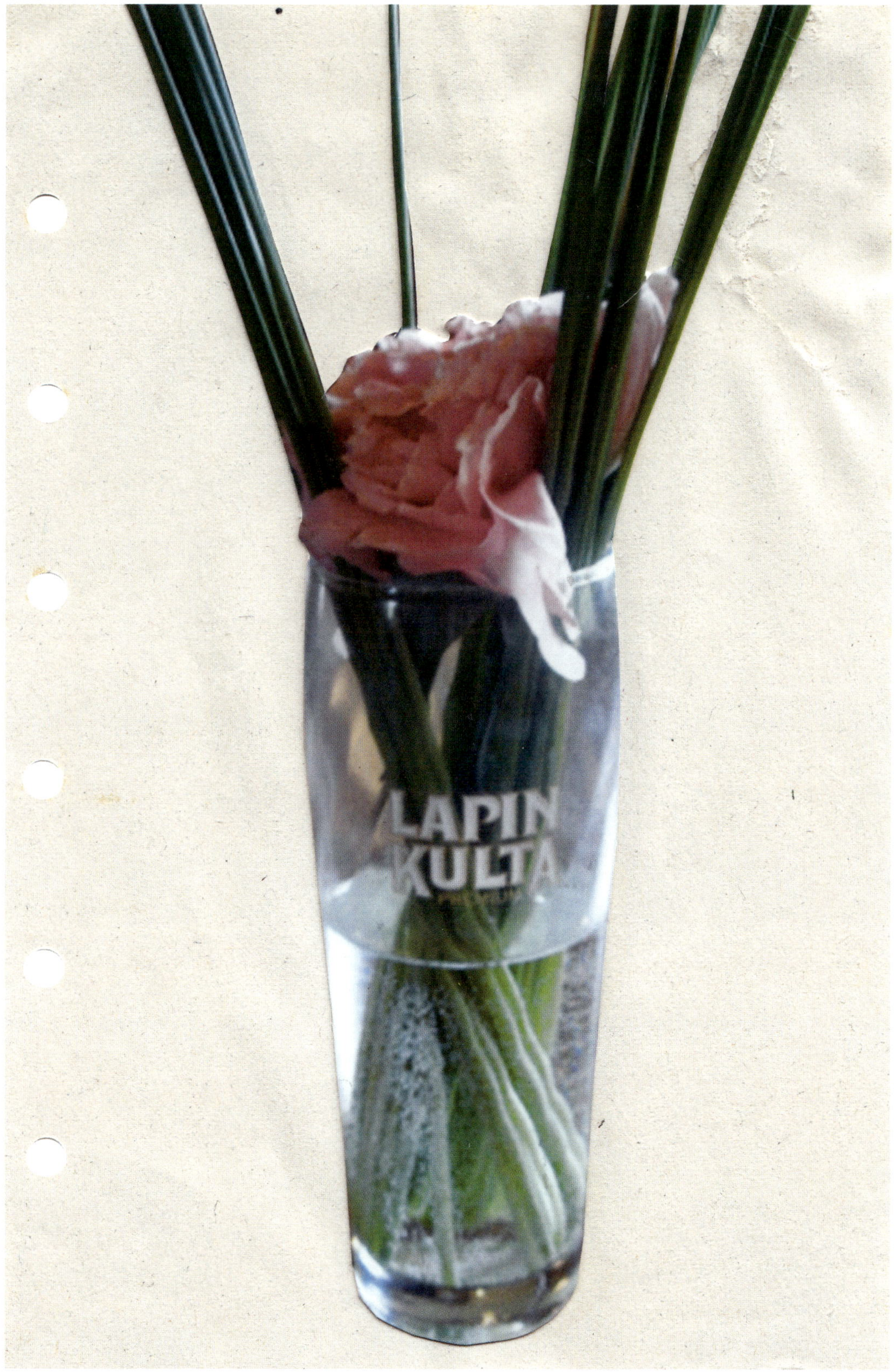

LAPIN
KULTA

HUGGING PEOPLE FROM BEHIND

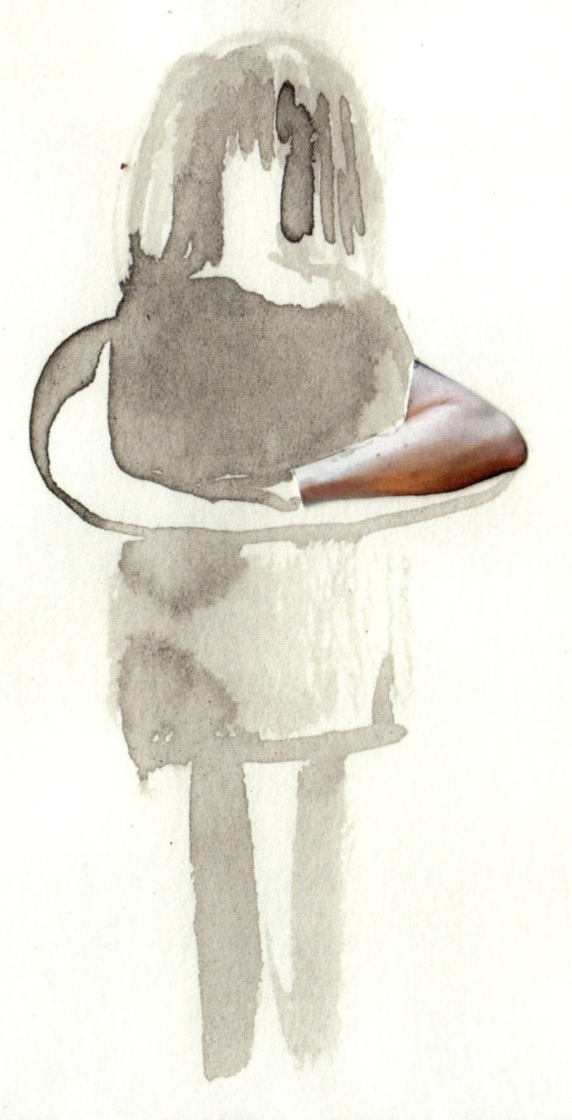

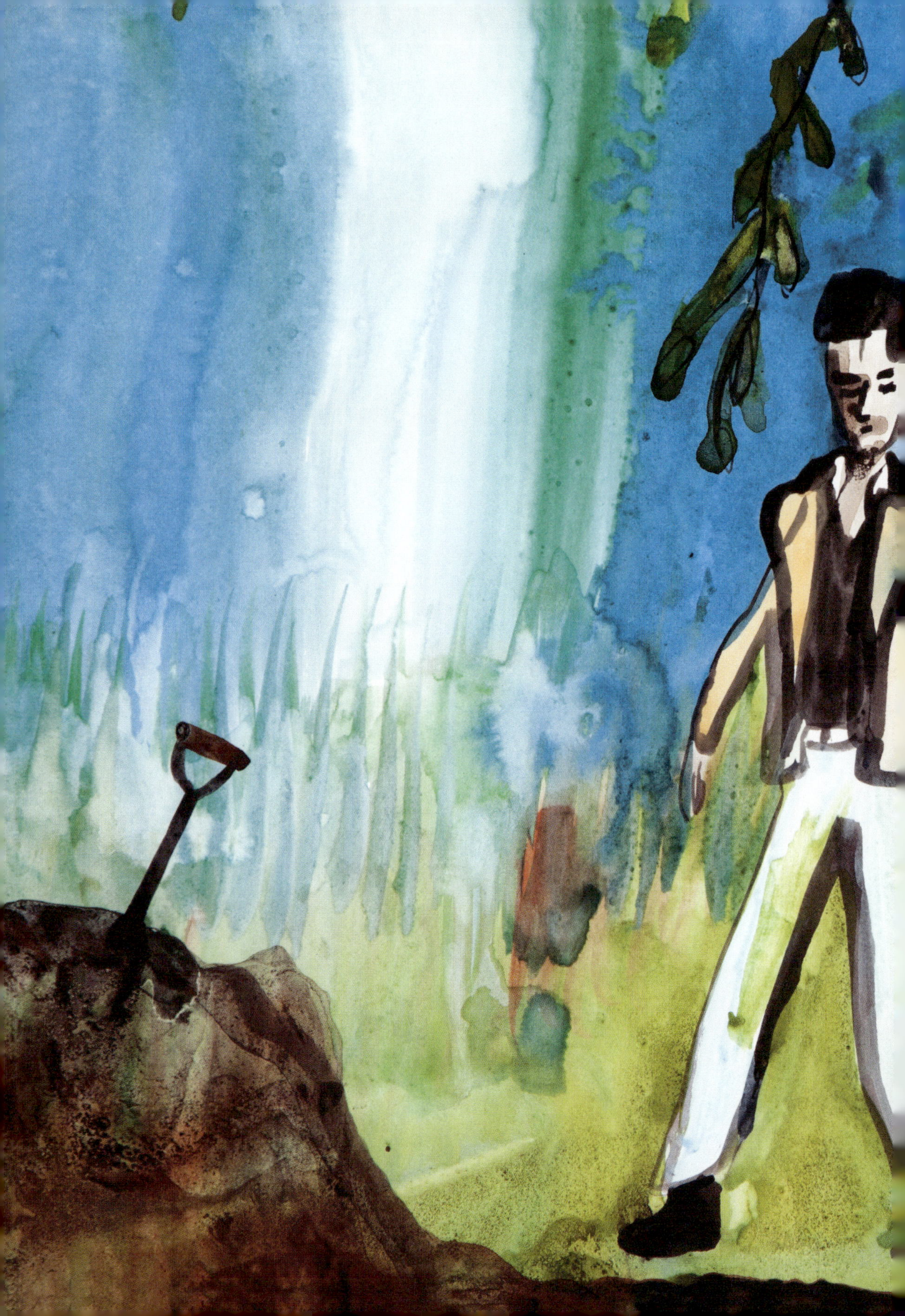

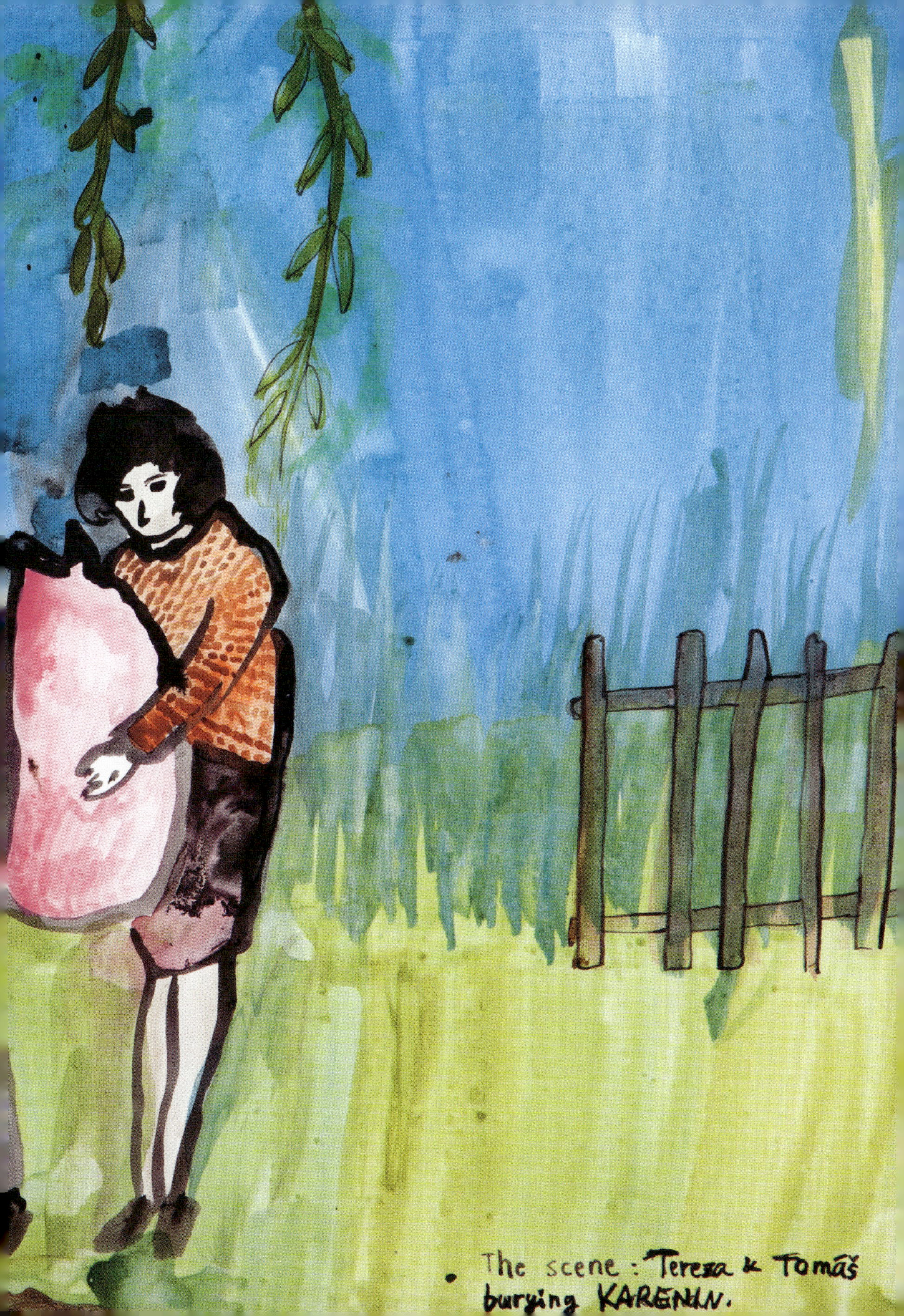

The scene : Tereza & Tomáš
burying KARENIN.

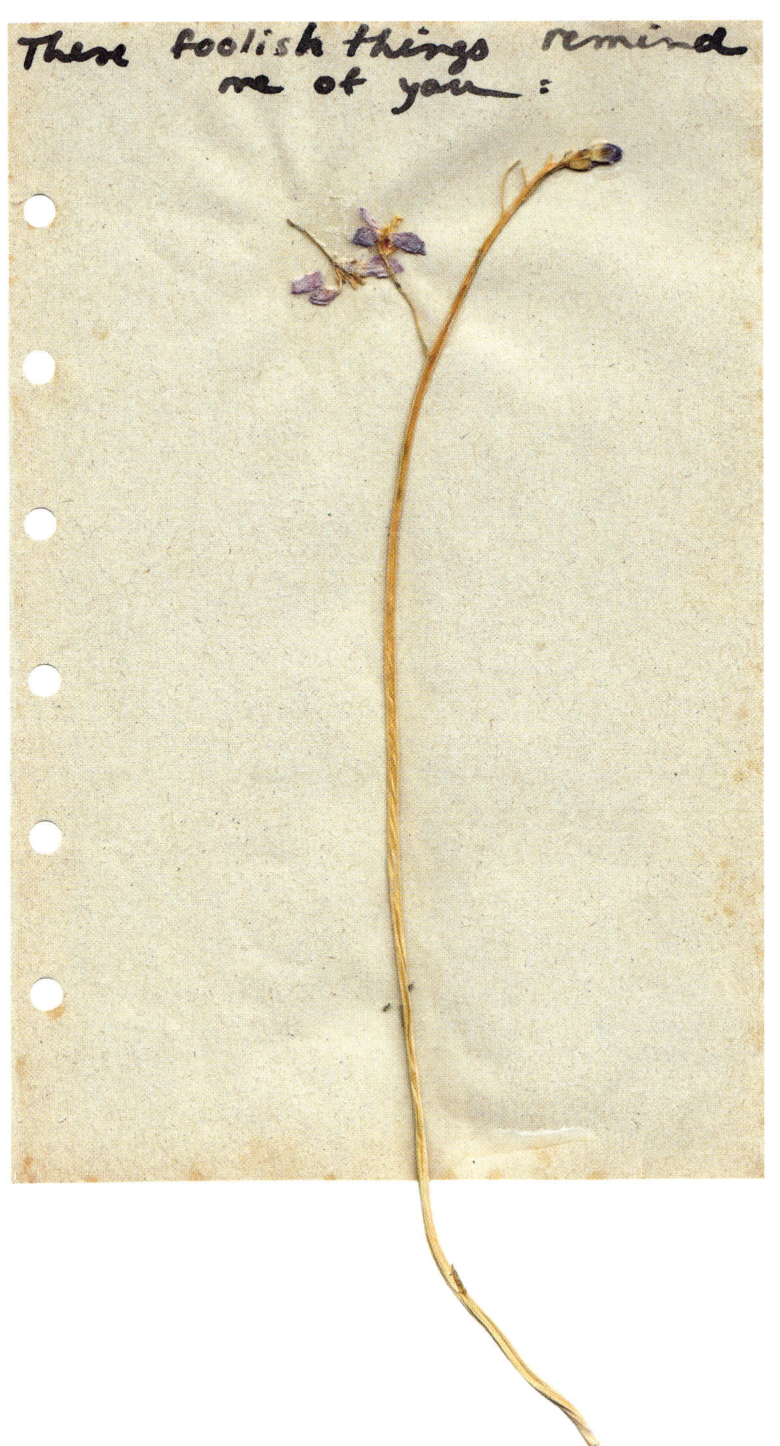

These foolish things remind
me of you:

BEAU-
TIFULLY
SHAPED
UPPER
ARMS

GÖTTER-SPEISE

FOOD OF THE GODS

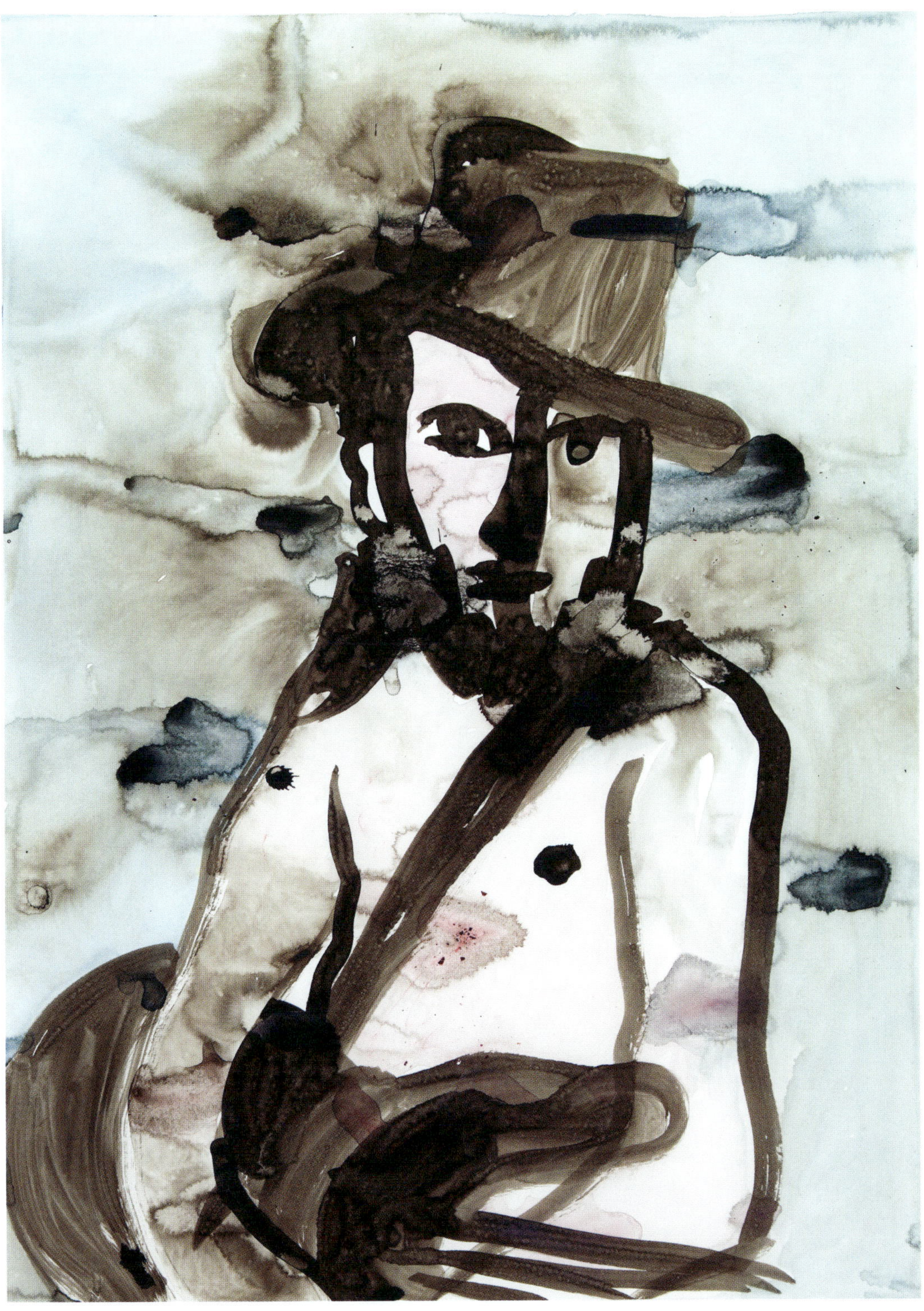

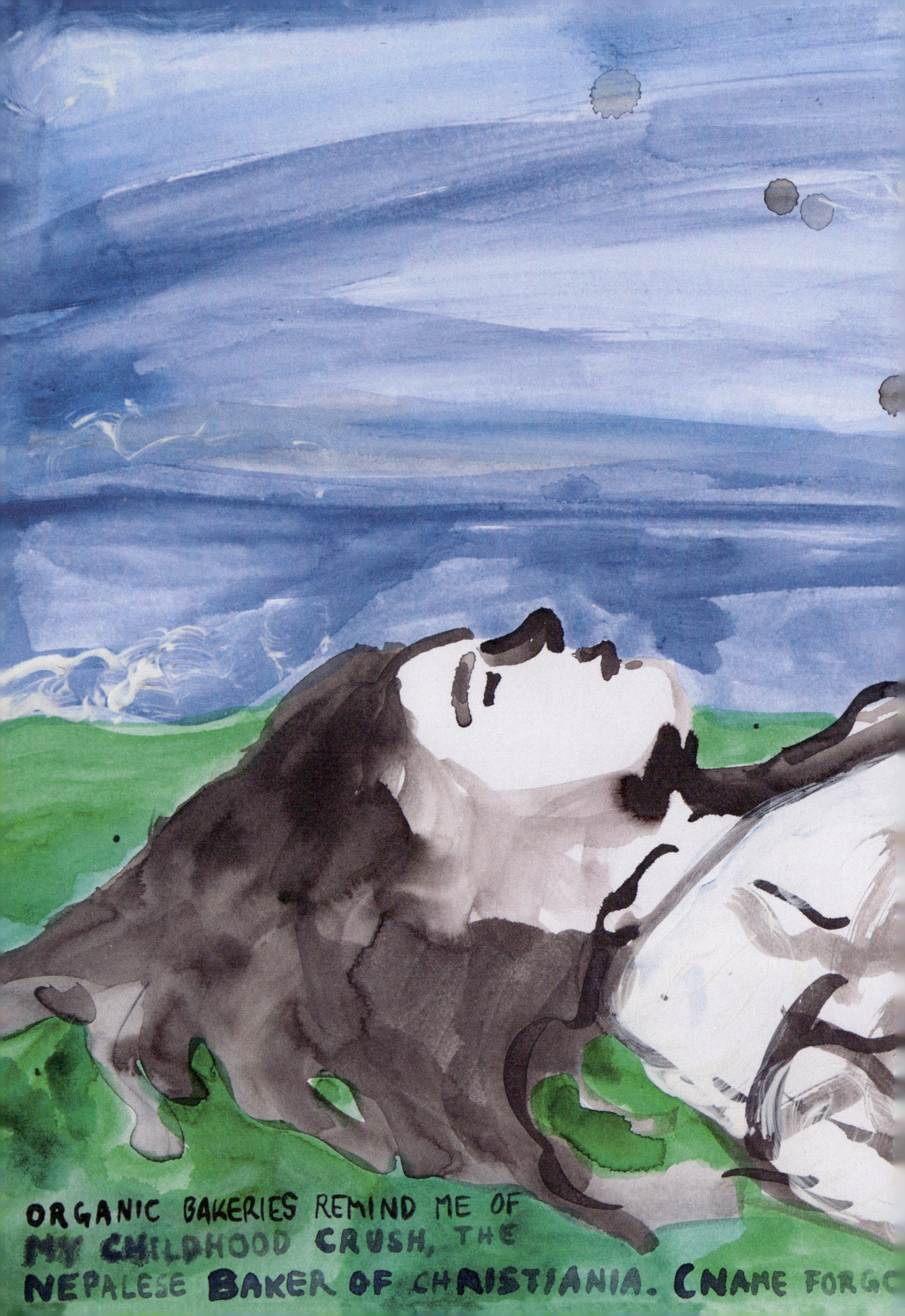
ORGANIC BAKERIES REMIND ME OF
MY CHILDHOOD CRUSH, THE
NEPALESE BAKER OF CHRISTIANIA. (NAME FORGO

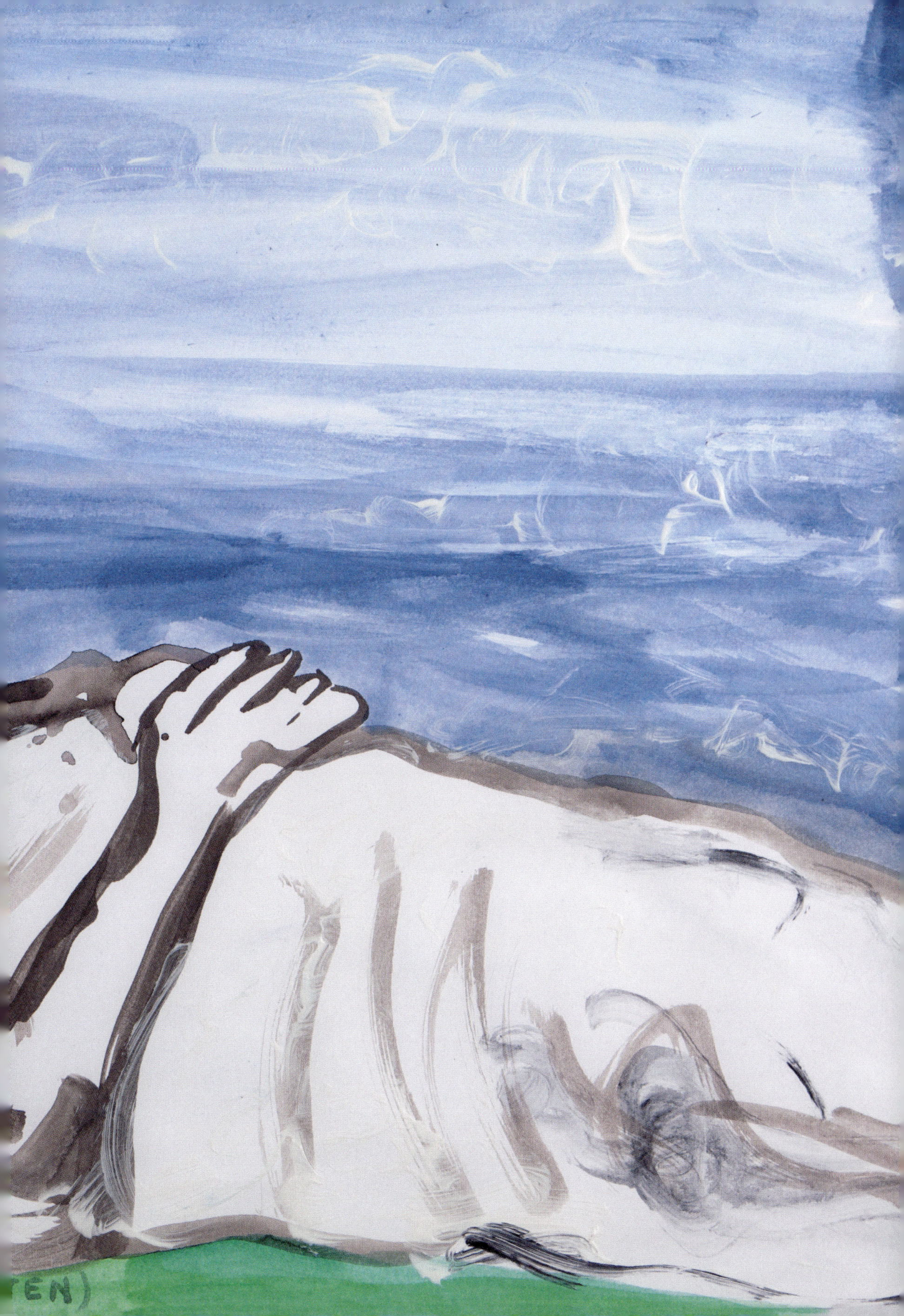
EN)

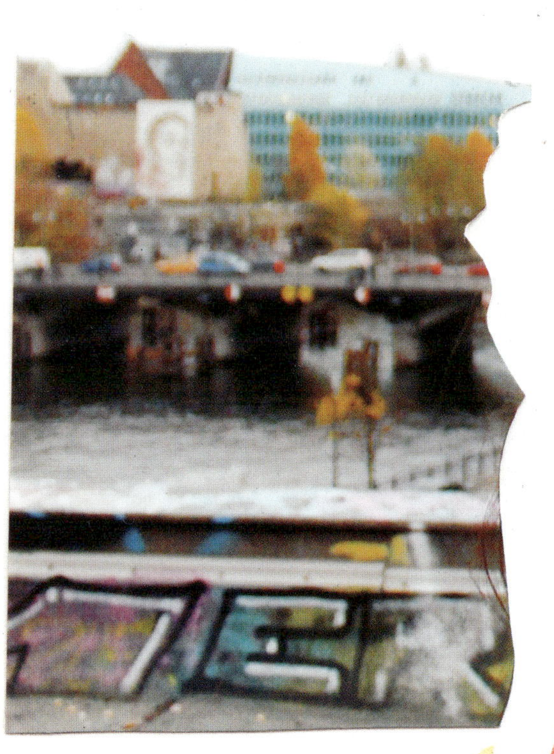

The Spree

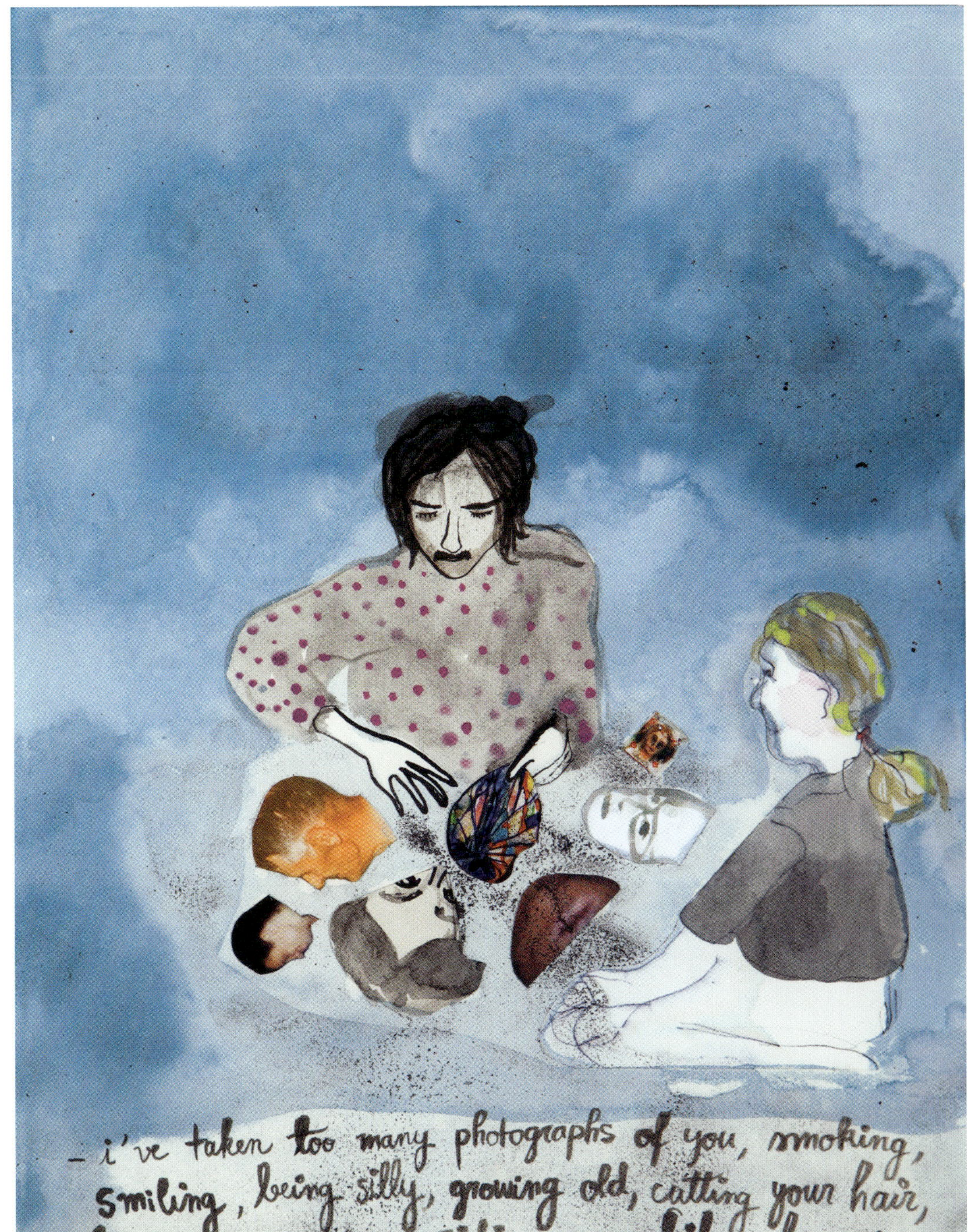

– i've taken too many photographs of you, smoking,
smiling, being silly, growing old, cutting your hair,
buying your cars, riding your bike, becoming
a man, looking at me ...

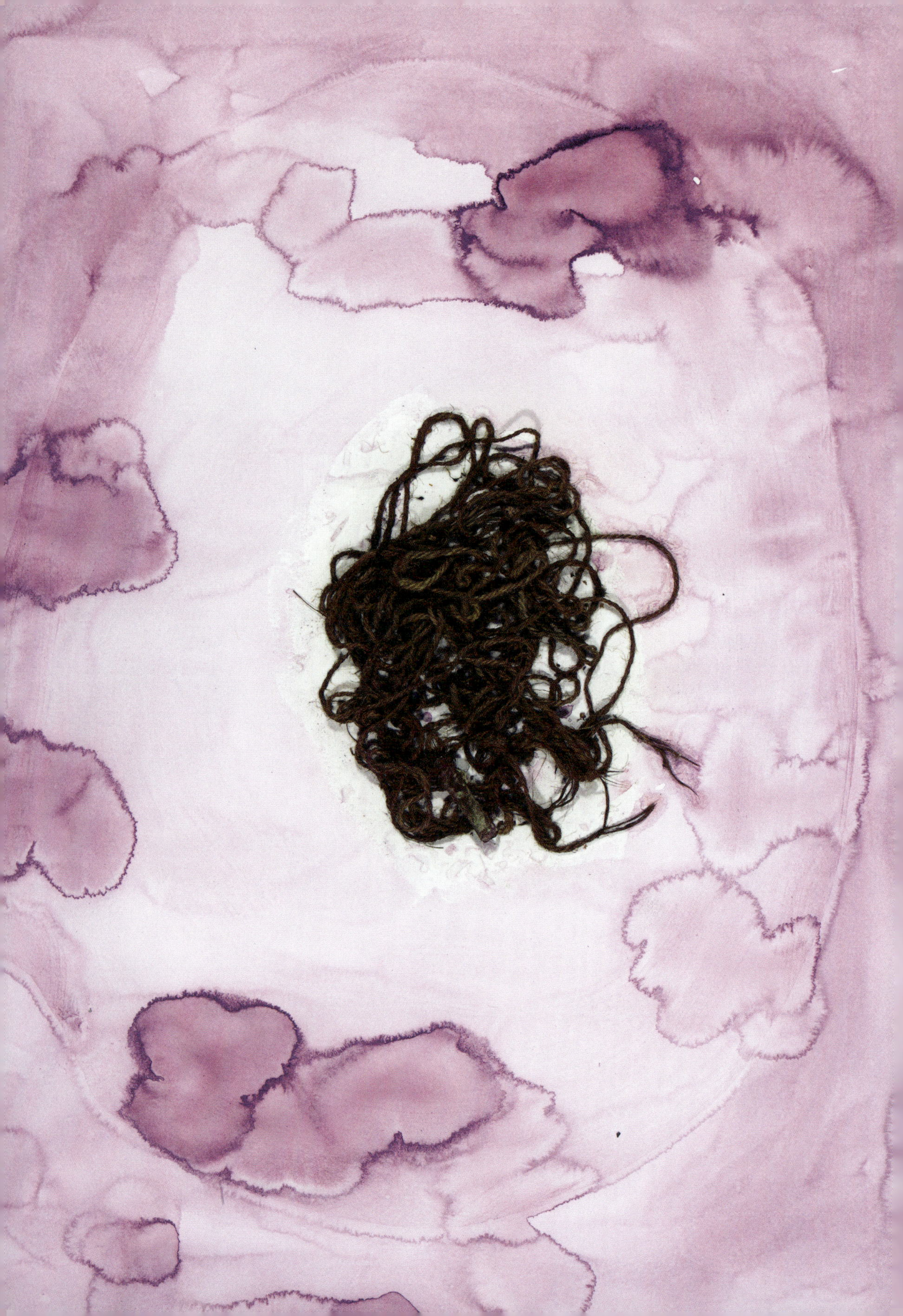

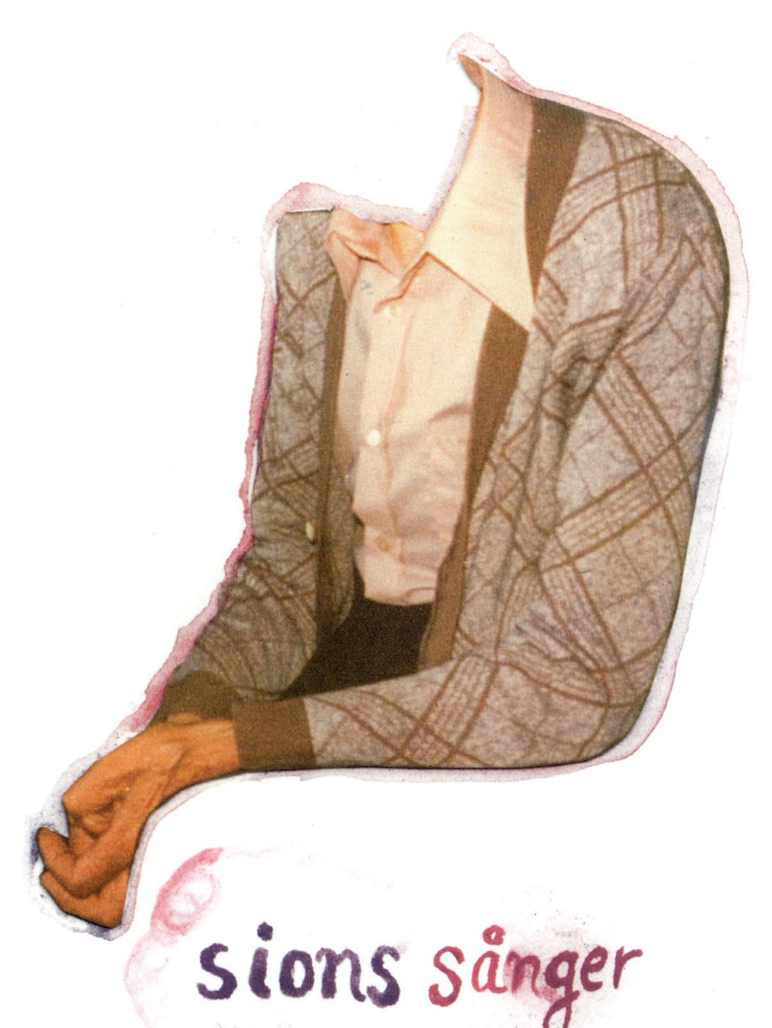

sions sånger

The verse :

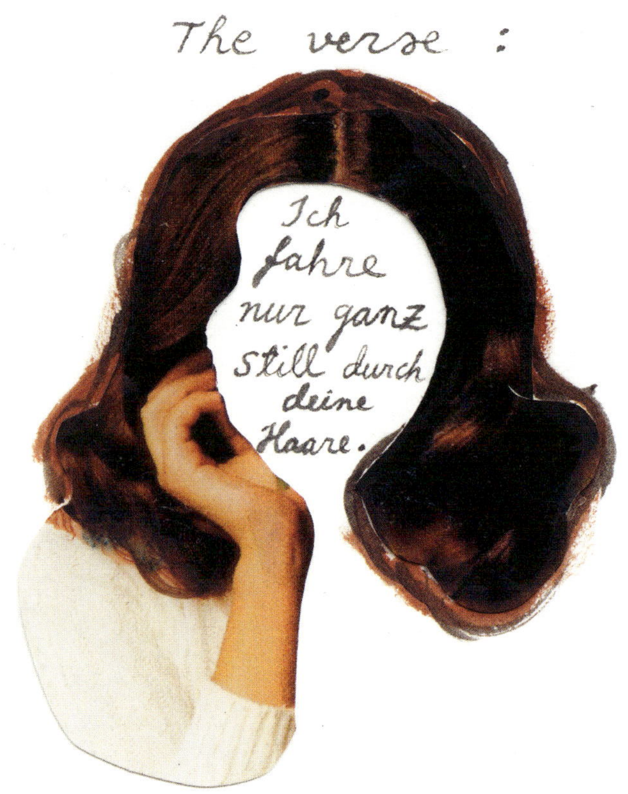
Ich
fahre
nur ganz
still durch
deine
Haare.

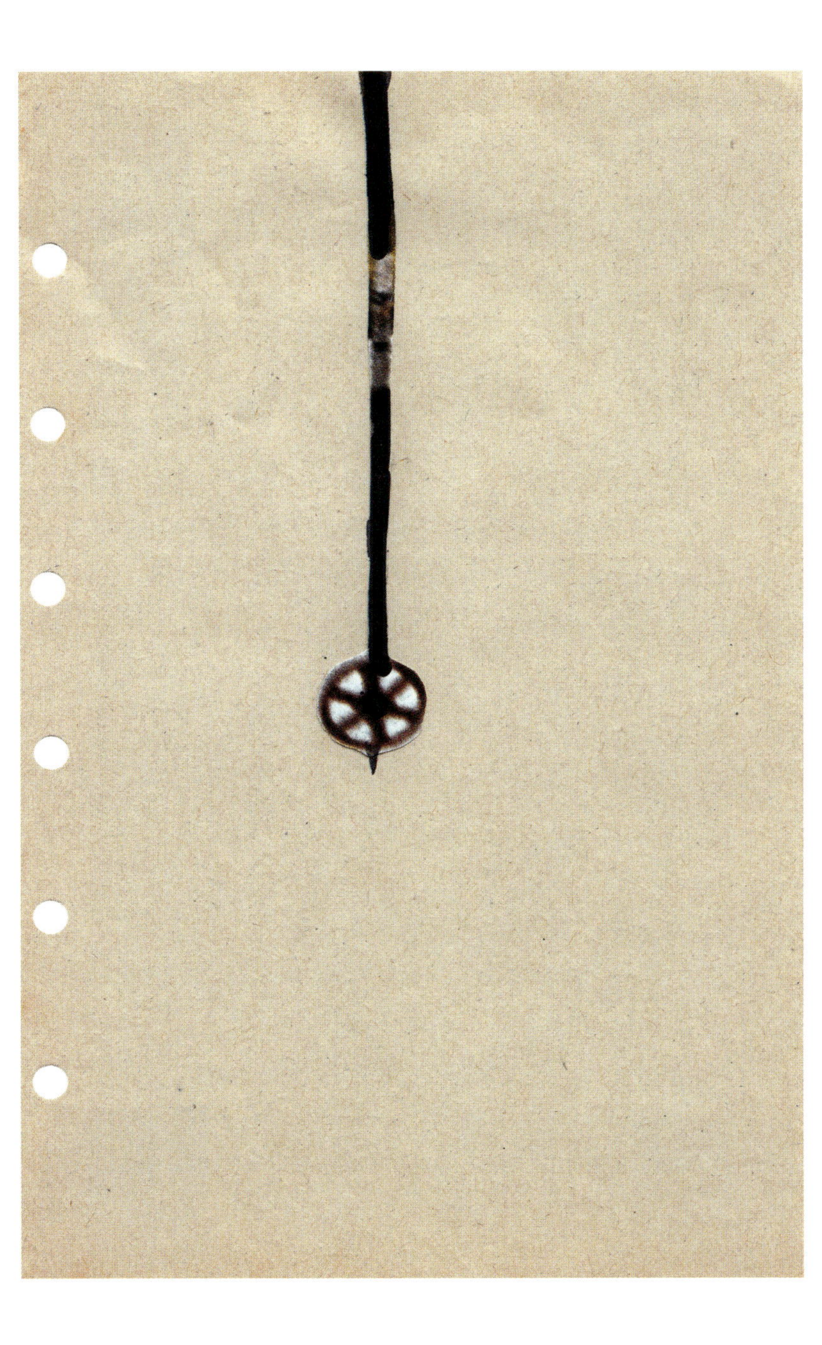

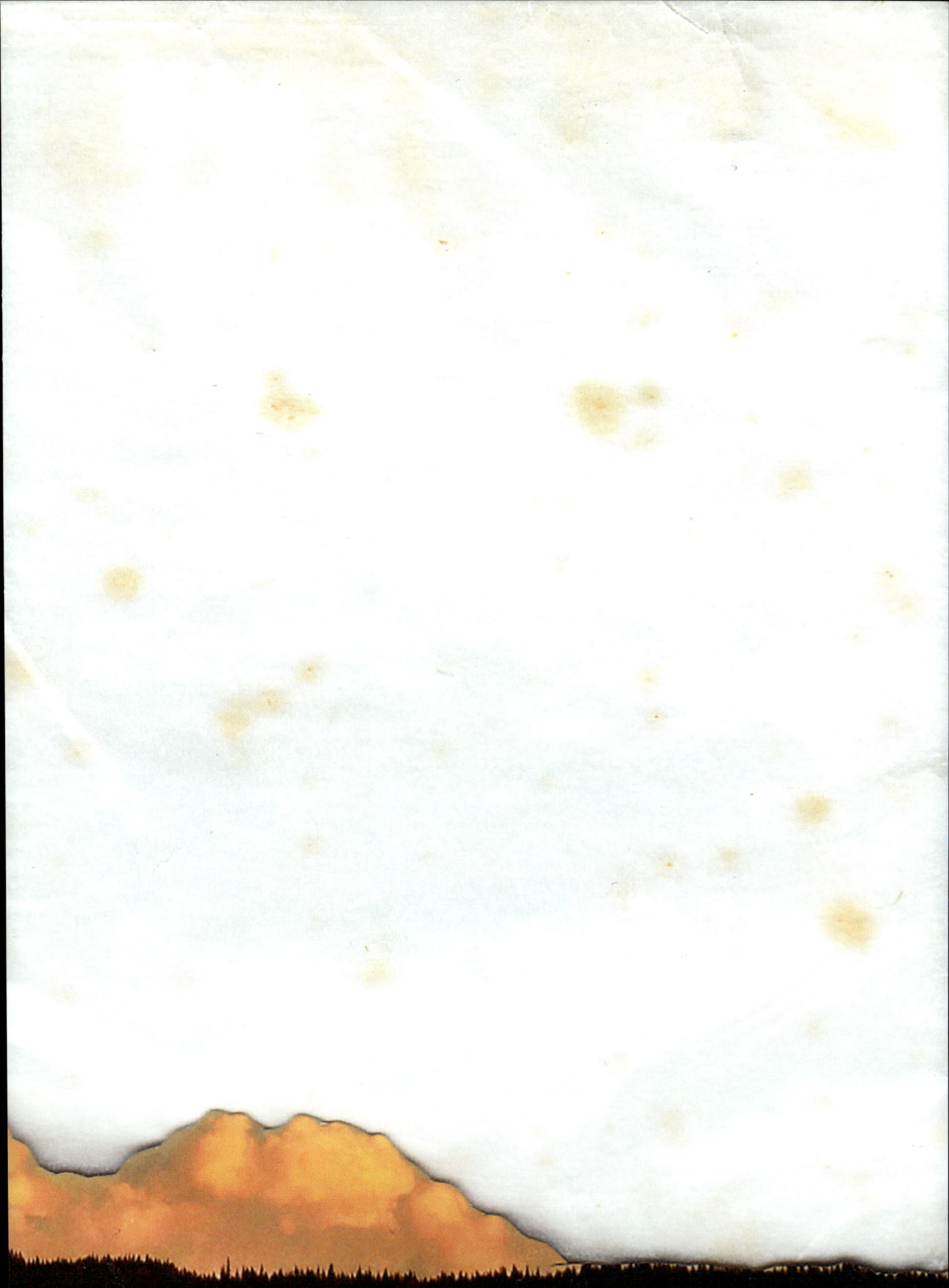

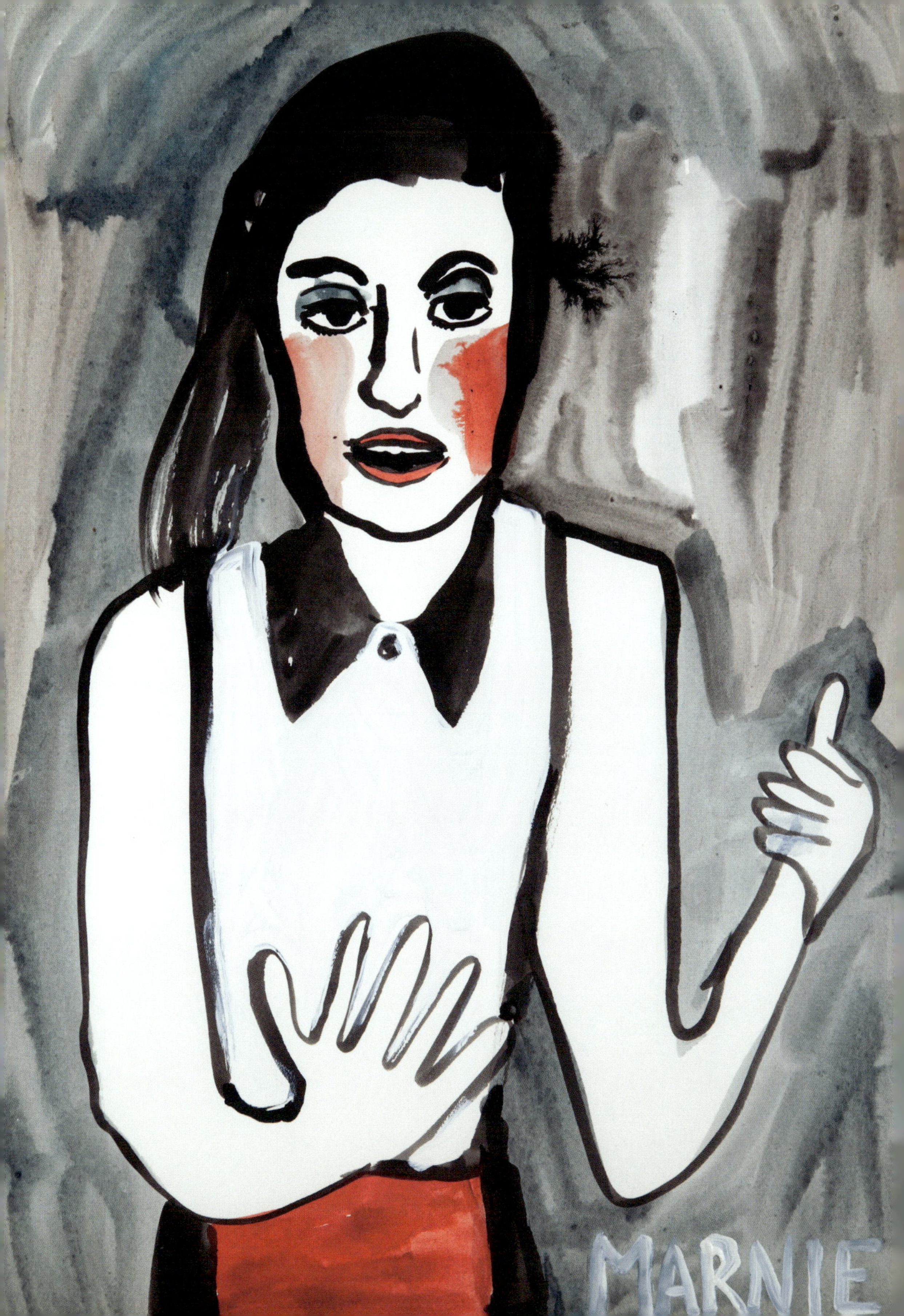
MARNIE

AND IT JUST PROVES TO ME, LIKE, IT DOESN'T MATTER HOW RIGHT YOU DO THINGS, BECAUSE YOU KNOW WHO END UP LIVING THEIR DREAMS ARE, LIKE, SAD MESSES LIKE CHARLIE. AND THE PEOPLE WHO END UP FAILING BEHIND ARE PEOPLE LIKE ME WHO HAVE THEIR SHIT TOGETHER

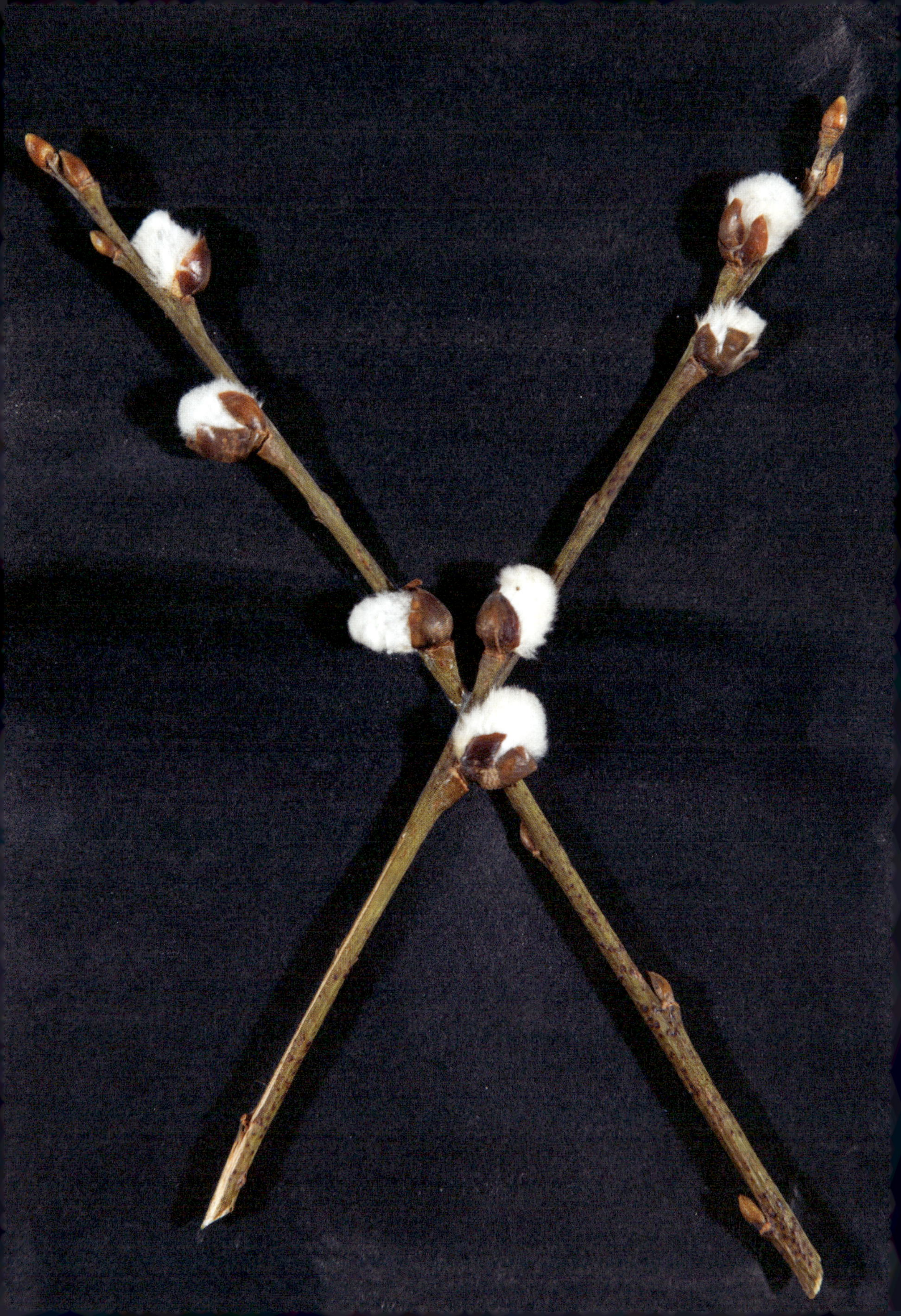

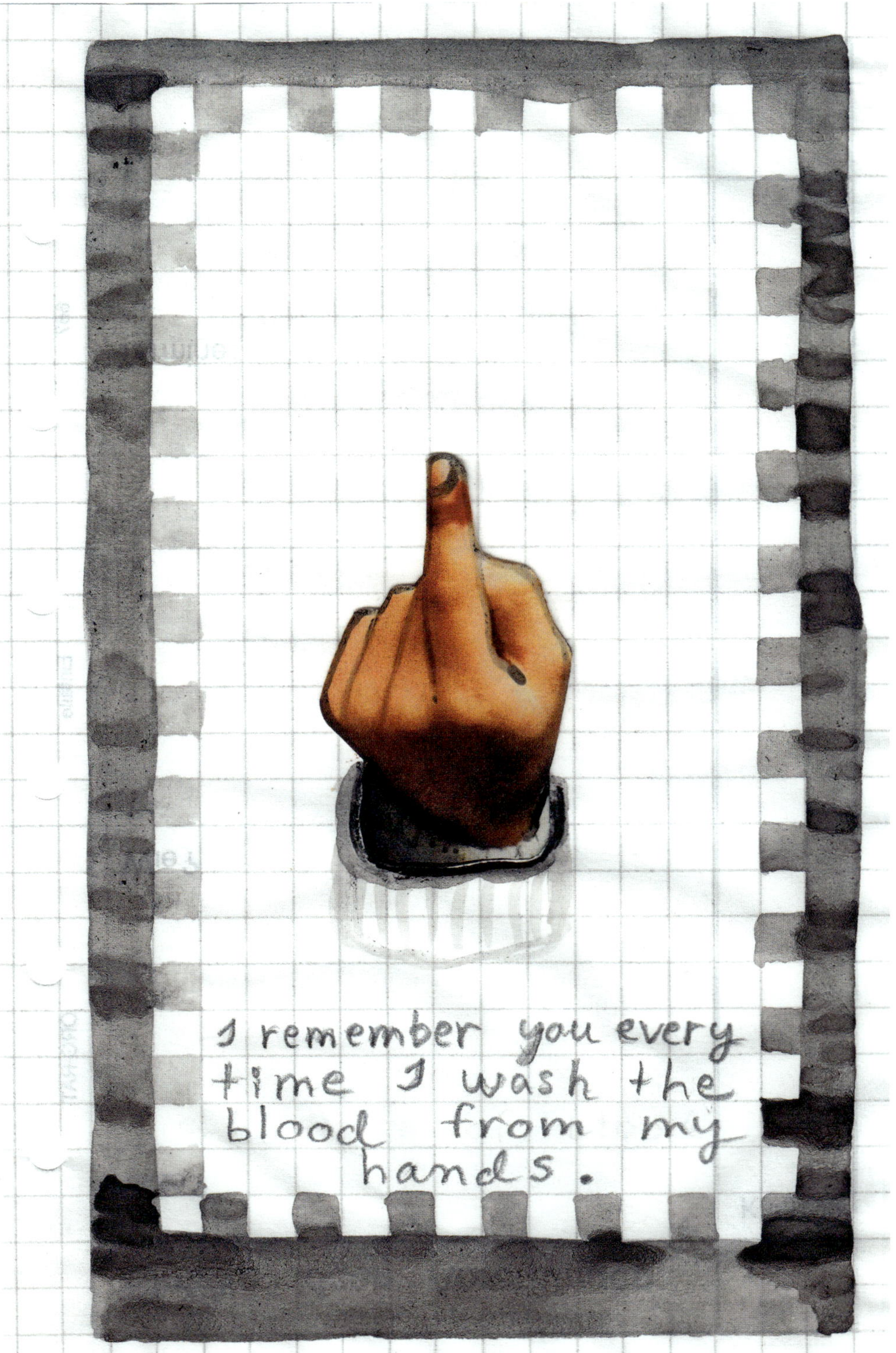

I remember you every time I wash the blood from my hands.

WE
WE'RE
MADE
IN THE
DARK

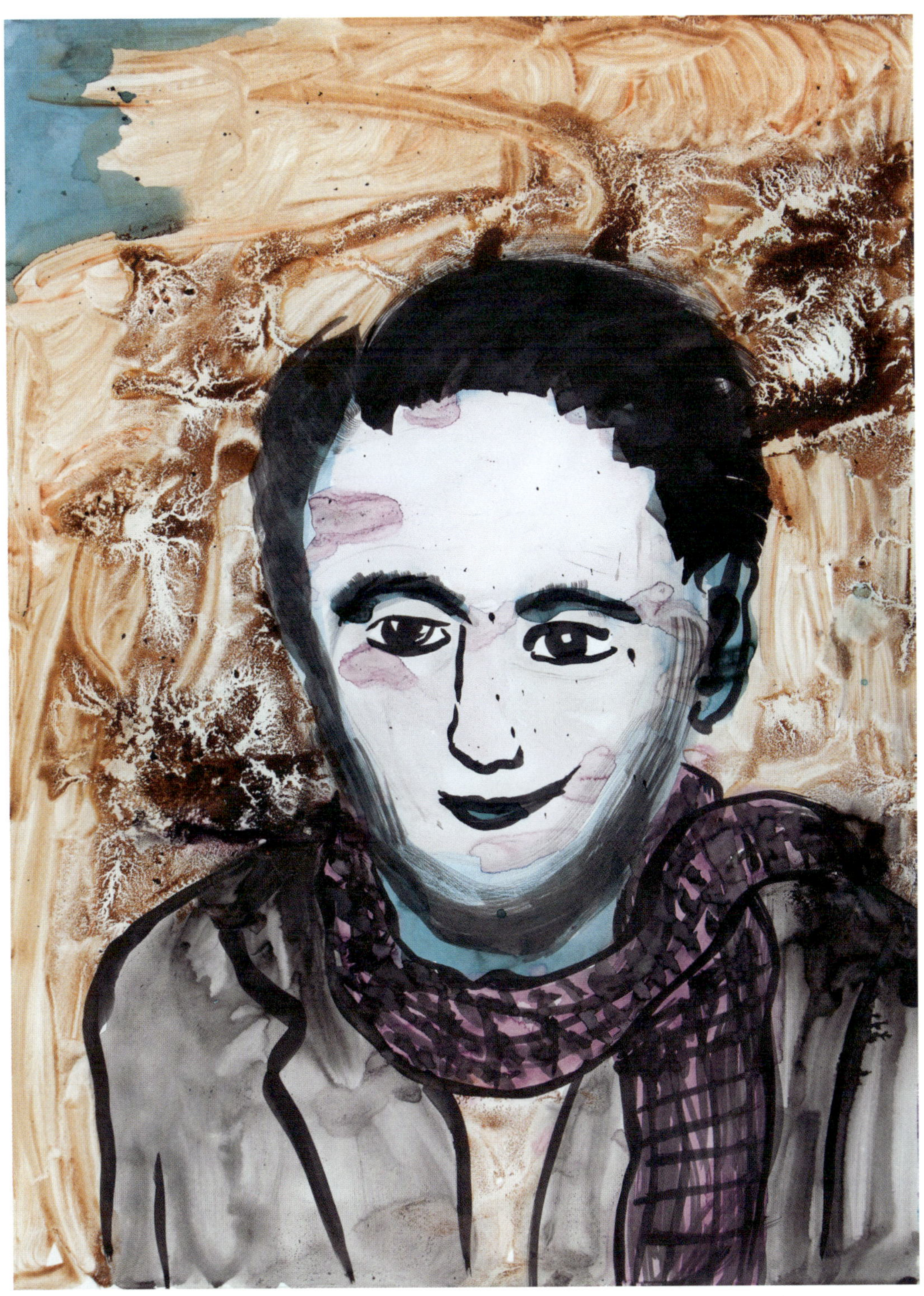

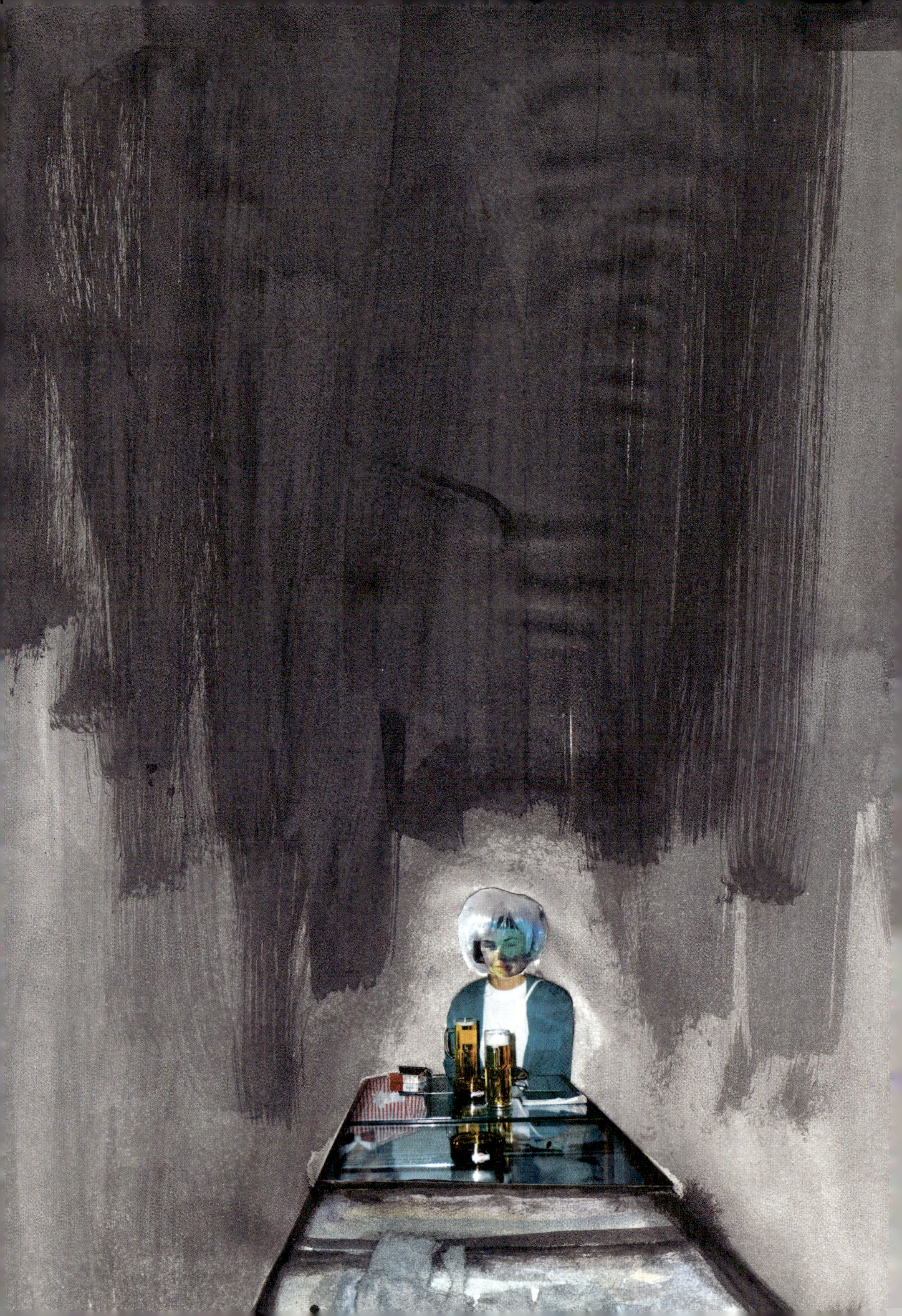

THE LYRICS
BY REMU:
"HYMYSI SUN, KUIN KAUNIS
KESÄTUULI, TÄHDEN-
LENNOKS KAIKKI
SITÄ LUULI"

(YOUR SMILE, LIKE
A BEAUTIFUL SUMMER
WIND, EVERYONE THOUGHT
IT WAS A FALLING STAR)

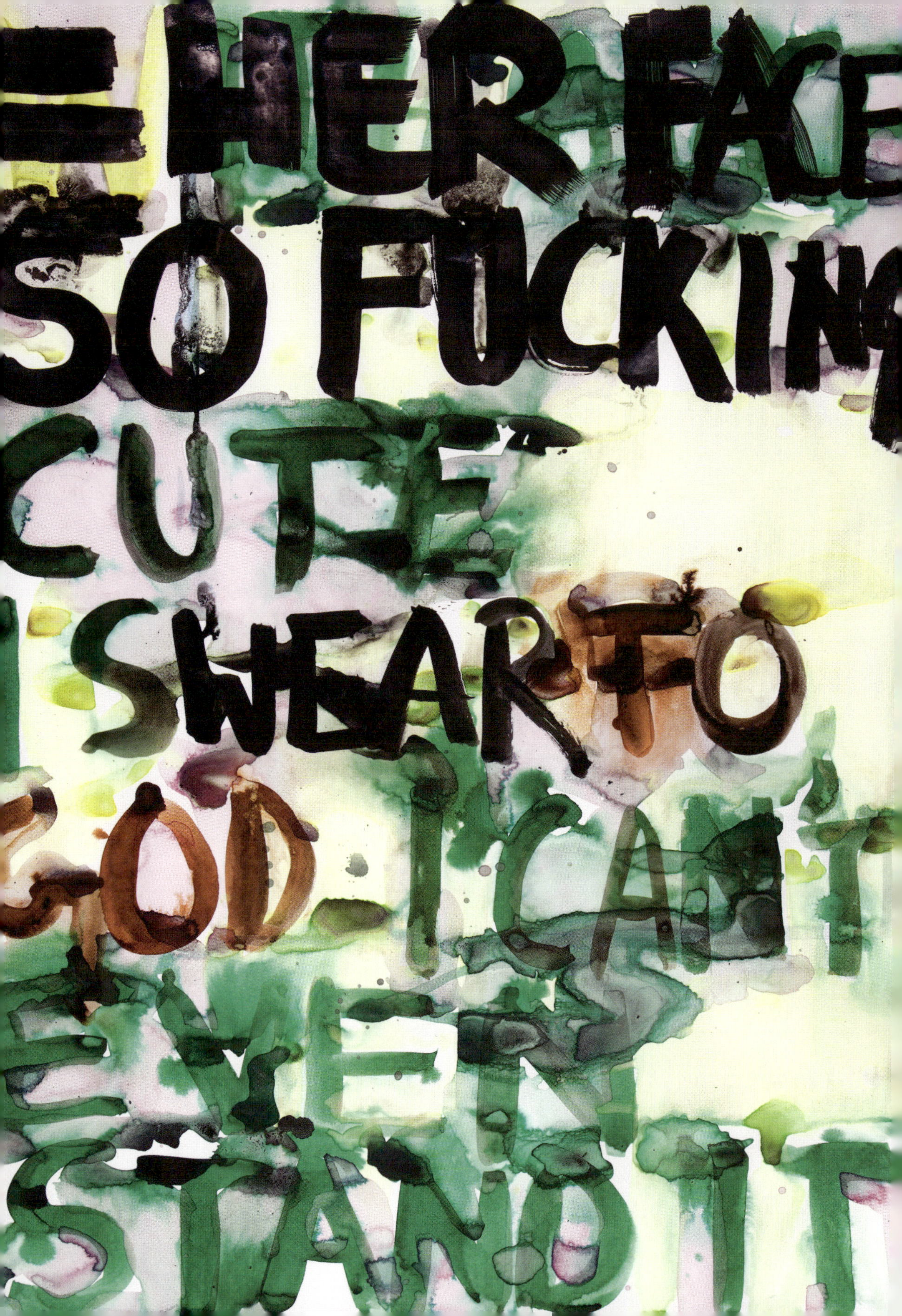

HER FACE
SO FUCKING
CUTE
I SWEAR TO
GOD I CAN'T
EVEN
STAND IT

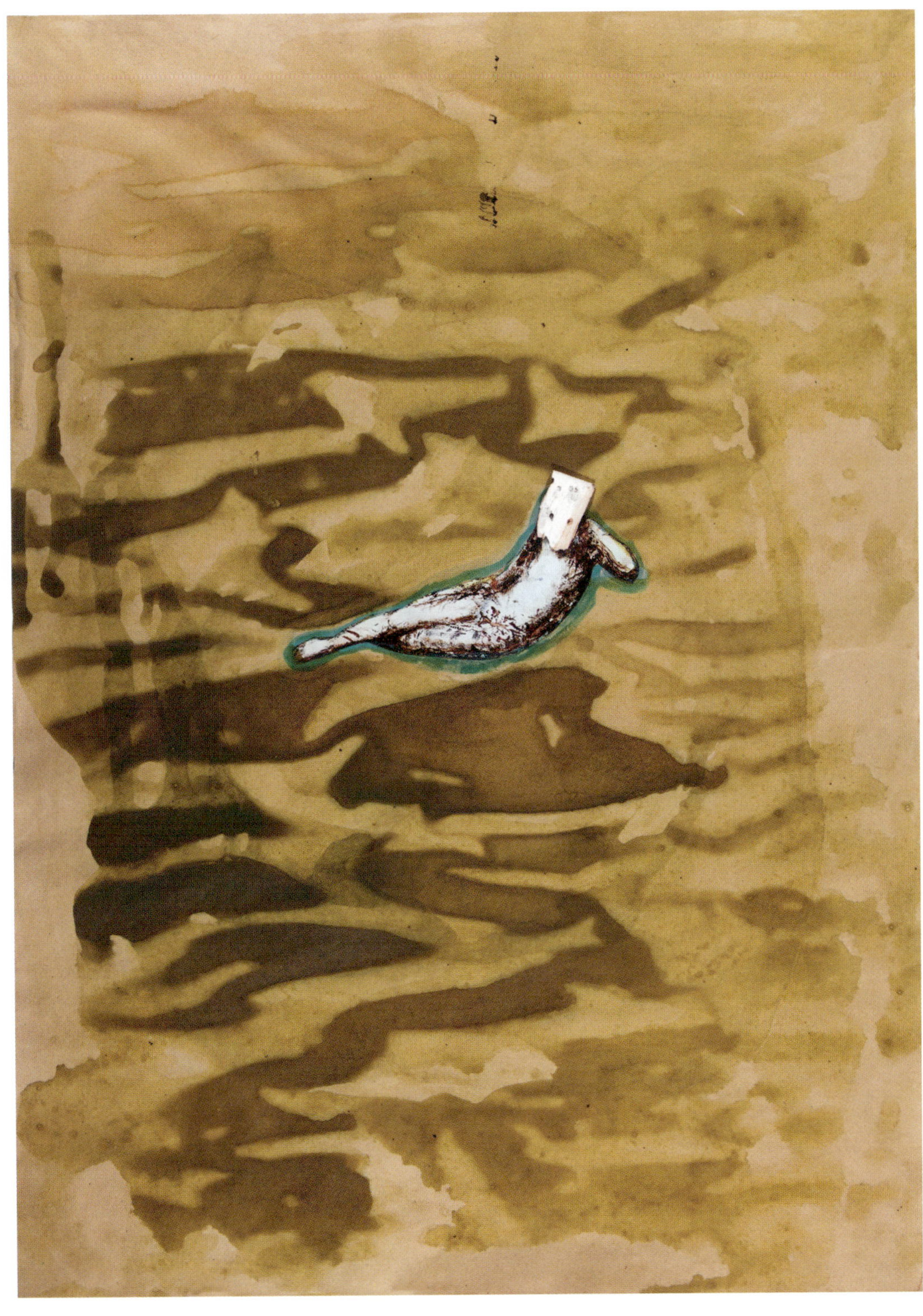

THAT SONG BY DEFTONES

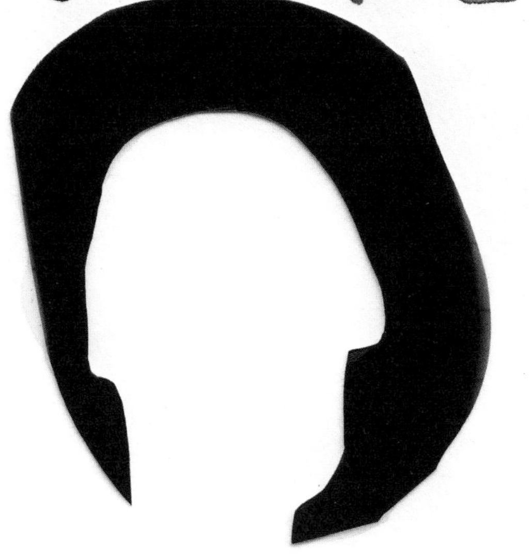

AND EVERYTHING BY THE CURE (WHICH I CAN'T LISTEN TO ANYMORE)

These Foolish Things Remind Me of You is a project by the artist Niina Lehtonen
Braun. In 2014, she began inviting friends and attendees of her exhibitions to
share things that remind them of someone special; anything from objects, lyrics,
or smells to situations. In response, she created over five hundred paintings,
drawings and collages, a selection of which is compiled in this volume. Her first
book *Mother Said* was published in 2013.

IMPRINT

CONCEPT & IMAGES
Niina Lehtonen Braun 2014–2016

EDITORS
Niina Lehtonen Braun & Christina Kral

DESIGN
Christina Kral

TRANSLATIONS & PROOFREADING
Tamerlane Camden-Dunne

THANK YOU
Ulu Braun, Thomas Wendrich, Franziska Böhmer,
Agnes Domke, Anne Euramaa, Sanna Isto, Tellervo
Kalleinen, Thomas Kilpper, Yves Mettler, Kirsi
Mikkola, Mika Minetti, Franzi and Hubert Moos,
Patrick Morarescu, Benjamin Müller, Katja Müller,
Pasi Mäkelä, Mirka Raito, Mimosa Pale, Janaina
Pessoa, Emma Puikkonen, Theresa Stroetges,
Tuomas Timonen, Teemu Tuonela, Simo Vassinen
and everyone who so generously shared and
contributed their memories and associations
for this project.

THIS PUBLICATION HAS BEEN MADE
POSSIBLE WITH THE KIND SUPPORT OF
Kone Foundation
Frame Contemporary Art Finland
Arts Promotion Centre Finland

The Deutsche Nationalbibliothek lists this
publication in the Deutsche Nationalbibliografie;
detailed bibliographic data are available on the
Internet at http://dnb.dnb.de.

Printed and published by: Kerber Verlag, Bielefeld
Windelsbleicher Str. 166–170, 33659 Bielefeld,
Germany

Tel. +49 (0)521 95 00 810
Fax +49 (0)521 95 00 888
info@kerberverlag.com

Kerber, US Distribution D.A.P.,
Distributed Art Publishers, Inc.
155 Sixth Avenue, 2nd Floor
New York, NY 10013
Tel. +1 (212) 627-1999
Fax +1 (212) 627-94 84

Kerber publications are available in selected
bookstores and museum shops worldwide
(distributed in Europe, Asia, South and North
America).

ISBN 978-3-7356-0291-6
www.kerberverlag.com

Printed in Germany